WHO'S BOSS?

TRAINING CHILDREN
IN SELF-MANAGEMENT
SECOND EDITION

FRANCIS H. WISE, PH.D.

WISE PUBLISHING COMPANY
wiselearntoread.com
WOODLAND HILLS, CALIFORNIA

WHO'S BOSS?
TRAINING CHILDREN
IN SELF-MANAGEMENT
SECOND EDITION

FRANCIS H. WISE, PH.D.

Editor: Joyce Wise

Copyright © 1982 Francis H. Wise, Ph.D.
Copyright © 2017 Joyce Wise
ISBN: 13: 978-0-915766-78-9
ISBN: 10: 0-915766-78-7
Library of Congress #82-91074

PREFACE

Who's Boss? was written for parents and educators by Dr. Francis H. Wise in 1982. His theories in training children in self-management were the result of many years spent in his office as a psychologist talking to parents, children, teenagers, and couples. It is his hope that adults and educators will begin to understand how much skill and knowledge is required to be a parent. He developed a system his clients could relate to called The PALE System of Habits. Through trial and error he discovered that every habit is composed of four systems — physical, authority relationships, language, and emotions — to develop a habit.

This updated version of *Who's Boss?* is geared for parents and educators, incorporating Dr. Wise's basic theories and ideas. It includes material on how to use The PALE System of Habits when learning new subjects and skills to become a successful adult. It also includes techniques to better understand the Framework of Self-Management. There is a reorganization of materials to reflect current attitudes For easy reference of the voluminous material presented, see the Index.

AUTHOR

Francis H. Wise, psychologist, practiced in Los Angeles, Sherman Oaks, and Thousand Oaks, California, for many years as a psychotherapist. He counseled many parents, children of all ages, couples (married and divorced), and businessmen with various personal and family problems over the years.

Dr. Wise has degrees in education, religion, sociology, psychology, and social studies. He attended Willamette University, Oregon College of Education, Oregon State, University of Oregon, Burton University, Harvard University, Union Theological Seminary, Oberlin Theological Seminary, University of the Philippines in Manila, University of Southern California, University of California Los Angeles, and University of Illinois.

Dr. Wise taught Sunday school classes since he was a teenager in Oregon. After graduating from the University of Oregon, he received his masters degree at USC, and from Burton University, a doctor's degree in psychology. He worked in the three largest churches in Los Angles doing all kinds of youth activities. He was a Chaplain in the United States Air Force for seven years and spent thousands of hours counseling hospital patients and those in the stockade. He was with the Armed Forces in Japan, Korea, Vietnam, and the Philippines where he received a second Doctorate in Psychology.

Dr. Wise taught grade school, high school and college classes, holding credentials as an elementary and high school teacher in both California and Oregon.

For the Boy Scouts of America, Dr. Wise was a cub master, scoutmaster, explorer and advisor. He wrote and produced a radio show for a year in Texas for the Boy Scouts of America. He spent four summers as a craft instructor as well as an assistant camp director for the boys camp in Vermont, a Y.M.C.A. Camp in Virginia, and at Camp Allegheny in West Virginia.

Dr. Wise authored Youth & Drugs, printed by Associated Press, 1973. He also authored a reader series for four and five year olds, entitled, *Dr. Wise Learn to Read Series* and an *Arithmetic Series for beginners.*

Joyce Wise majored in book publishing at UC Northridge. She designed and published with her husband the famous *Learn to Read Series* and *Arithmetic Series For Beginners.* Joyce then authored two storybooks for second graders, *Musette Finds A Friend* and *Musette & Pierre's Family* along with two beginning grammar books, *Ann's Rebels* and *Ann Goes To School.* She has rewritten and updated *Who's Boss?*, her husband's life's work, for all to enjoy.

Franklin Wise redesigned and engineered this updated version of *Who's Boss?* to reflect today's attitudes. He graduated from the University of Santa Barbara with a Bachelor of Science in psychology and is also a successful programming engineer.

ACKNOWLEDGMENTS

Thank you Katalin Joo, my Desktop Publishing teacher, who patiently taught me Illustrator and InDesign. It was her thorough knowledge and skill as a teacher that made this publication possible. When I wanted to quit, she gave me the courage to fight through the difficult tasks of perfecting my skill towards a more professional look. Thank you Kata.

Thank you to Karen Robbins, my art and Photoshop teacher, who brought me into the world of designing art. Without her confidence in me and her expertise in design, I would not have succeeded. Yes, Karen, I was listening when you lectured.

NOTES

All names used throughout this book are fictitious and any resemblances are purely coincidental.

The universal 'he' is used instead of 'he' and 'she,' in order to avoid awkwardness for the reader.

TABLE OF CONTENTS

Gratitude is the spice of life.
It is the pleasant glow of the candle of love
that dispels greed, hate, self-serving, and loneliness.

PART I - THE 5 AUTHORITY RELATIONSHIPS

Chapter 1

Who's Boss?

The Little King

One day Dr. Wise, while shopping at the market for his wife, heard a six-year-old acting like a "little king." He stood rigidly, with chest thrown out, demanding his way.

"Mom, I want this!" he demanded and plopped a toy into the grocery cart.

"I am sorry, son, but we cannot buy this now," his mother replied as she placed the toy back on the shelf.

A look of frustration and bewilderment came over the "little king's" face as he blurted out, "No! No! I want it! I want it now!"

"Stop making a scene!" pleaded his mother.
"You can't make me!" shouted the six-year-old.

Finally his mother had had enough and told him bluntly, "This has got to stop! You do this to me every time we go shopping!"

Shocked, the "little king" became enraged as if he had been royally insulted and an injustice had been done to him. Very loudly he shouted at the top of his voice, "You are selfish and stingy, and I'm going to tell Daddy on you!"

1

Chapter 1

As Dr. Wise stood watching the "little king" shower his mother with embarrassing accusations, he did not once noticed Dr. Wise or the couple standing close by.

Finally, his mother could take it no longer. She grabbed his little hand and pulled him along shaking her head. Dr. Wise could tell she was upset and bewildered as she blurted out "Who's Boss? You or me?"

Does this episode sound familiar? Many parents experience similar situations which challenge parental authority. Parents wonder what they have done to deserve such nasty treatment from a child they love so dearly. Mother especially receives the brunt of the "little king's" infantile behavior as she spends endless hours alone caring for her child.

Puzzled, mother becomes anxious, upset, and frightened trying to work out a solution to "Who's Boss?" As a last resort she turns to father for help.

But father, too, frequently finds himself anxious and upset in the "little king's" torture chamber. Being a first-time parent, without experience or idea on how to train a child out of demanding ways, father turns the burden of responsibility completely over to mother. His excuse is that this is not a masculine duty. This, of course, doesn't solve the difficulty, as father places mother in a more frustrating and helpless position. Mother now feels alone and rejected by her husband and child. Both parents generally continue to suffer daily from a demanding child.

Thus, the family unity is broken. Mother feels alone while father drops out of parenting, to both father's and child's detriment. Eventually, both parents have feelings of rejection as their child continues to grow in his demands. The parents wonder how their child got to be so bossy.

Who's Boss?

A Cry For Survival

It all starts with the first hungry cry of the newborn infant. The infant is endowed with a magnificent protection to call mother's and father's attention to him when he needs service because of his helplessness.

Parents intuitively respond the first time they hear a helpless cry for attention. Yes, they are right to rapidly respond to the infant's needs, as this cry is a call for survival.

Diapers are changed immediately. Every cry is answered instantly. From this first cry of need, mother and father become excellent parents to their infant.

It is also the beginning of the infant conditioning the parents to obey his every need. However, mother and father do not view this immediate attention as being conditioned to obey the infant's every need. In fact, they are delighted to see their infant smile, wave his little fat fists or put his foot into his mouth.

The curiosity of the infant is a wonder, which delight father and mother. They are infatuated in witnessing his development as he grows in length and weight. So as the infant develops the ability to sleep longer, to eat more, to sit up and to crawl, he is becoming less helpless. Now, until that time, mother and father have little choice but to respond to their infant's every need.

Eventually, mother gets used to her infant's movements, his types of cries and sounds, not only at night but during the day, since she is with him most of the time. From experience, mother learns to determine which cries are for attention and which cries are for help.

Now that mother can distinguish between cries for help and attention, she has a choice. She can now not respond, if she doesn't want to, without being anxious or frustrated.

Mother is learning to adjust to what is serious and what is just attention getting. She also learns to adjust to the growing experiences of her infant. Mother is catching on to the ways of her infant.

Yes, as long as the infant is helpless, mothers and fathers do not have a choice but to respond instantly to their little infant. However, it escapes many mothers and fathers' attention that their infant's cry is the beginning of learning to boss others for survival. As the infant becomes less helpless, mother and father must start training their child out of infantile ways. It is at this point, parents need to change.

Change? They are happy with baby as he is. Why should they change? Their infant is perfect as far as they are concerned.

Dethroning The King

As the infant becomes less helpless, he is no longer a newborn, but a growing, changing baby whose every demand doesn't need to be met instantly. He can now do many things for himself. Infantile behavior is no longer needed and the urgency to respond every time baby makes a demand needs to be diminished.

But, baby continues to draw the natural conclusions that he has the right to make demands as he did as a helpless newborn infant. This is true because he believes everything belongs to him. Do you remember the "little king" in the store didn't notice that anybody was watching him make a fool out of himself and, once more, he didn't care. That is because he thought he could still make demands as he did as an infant. This is a natural misconception that the child must be trained out of by his parents.

The truth is, no one has explained to the child that he can no longer demand what he doesn't need or he cannot demand what is not his.

In the meantime, mom and dad have become used to fulfilling the infant's every needs. They become so wrapped up in their child's continuous demands that they fail to recognize that baby does not need to have every demand met now. Both child and parents need to be trained out of responding immediately.

Changes In Authority Relationships

Parents are delighted when they see their infant become a baby who can now sit up, smile, and reach for things. His little personality is beginning to show. He is now sleeping through the night, and the dethroning of the "little king" must begin as he becomes less helpless.

One of the exciting moments for all parents is the first time baby stands up by himself. This is a big event for mom, dad, grandparents, aunts, uncles, neighbors and friends. Once baby can stand up, most parents cannot wait until he starts to walk. These two events are magnificent and wonderful experiences for all concerned. Unfortunately, many parents do not recognize the significance of these two events, as it changes many things in terms of future authority relationships.

Why Dethroning Is Important

These two events represent all kinds of delightful activities ahead for the parents and the child. But many parents fail to see that standing up is the beginning of a dramatic change in authority relationships between parent and child. Standing up is the beginning for the "little king" to discover there is more than one authority relationship. He will be dethroned, not only by his parents' authority, but by nature's. He tries desperately, at times, to keep his authority as it was before he stood up.

If parents do not dethrone their child, or if the dethroning process is unknown to them, they will be inept in teaching authority relationships when their child demands his own way and throws temper tantrums. This is why parents need to gradually dethrone the child.

Baby's Advantages

With first-time parents, baby is more likely to have the advantage in authority relationships. This is so as mom and dad are not too sure how to teach child management. If mom and dad do not solve the authority problem with child number one, child number two will still have the advantage until they understand how to use authority relationships to their advantage.

One reason why some first-time parents don't understand authority relationships is that they continue to meet baby's every demand, even though he has become less helpless and can do many things on his own. These parents ignore the fact that their child has had two years of experience in bossing them before they ever got a chance to verbally control him.

Learning to control others is a necessary experience to provide for one's needs as an infant. This is how baby escapes from the natural state of helplessness.

Baby is unaware of the several natural advantages he has in authority relationships.

Who's Boss?

First, he has no vocabulary, so he cannot be controlled by words for about fifteen months. The parents do, however, control baby to some extent with facial expressions, tones of voice, and physical methods.

Second, baby's advantage is that he cannot lose his privileges, and therefore punishment is ineffective.

Third, the first-born child has an advantage because his parents are inexperienced in child management.

Fourth, baby is more experienced in exercising his authority over his parents than the parents are over him. Therefore, the child may, for a longer period of time, remain the "king," until the parents figure out what is happening.

It is easy now to see how baby got the idea that he is boss. These misconceptions sometimes continue for many years.

How Does Baby Change?

Baby is constantly growing physically as well as mentally. When he can walk, explore, and say a few words, he can then learn many lessons on his own. The child, many times, learns the lessons of self-control that nature teaches faster than the lessons Mom teaches. This is because nature is constant and consistent. Many times mom is more lenient and not consistent enough for the child to learn self-control.

Don't misunderstand me, the parent is always controlling baby in many ways, which baby doesn't know is control. I suspect he doesn't even care. So it is easy and natural for him to draw the wrong conclusion about authority relationships.

Baby has no idea what the word "authority" means, although many adults mistakenly think he does and will hit

7

him thinking that he is defying adult authority.

Fathers stress obedience to authority more than mothers, and they, therefore, are more annoyed by baby's natural control of parents. Men have been taught both in military training as well as in their business activities the importance for authority and obedience.

Fathers, however, are correct in stressing authority, but many don't know that authority training cannot be taught to a child until age four or five. Father's ignorance of authority training for preschoolers then places him in conflict with mother, causing a disruptive family relationship. This adds to the difficulty of understanding "Who's Boss?"

There are naturally occurring times when mother and father can train their child in self-management, but these times are determined by the maturational levels of the child which will be discussed later in the book.

The Misconception Of Parents

The usual thought of parents and adults, in general, is that there is only one authority relationship; that is, the parent is boss at all times and must be obeyed. This is partially true but there are four more authority relationships which are equally as important. Every adult and child practices them every day, even though they are not aware that they are doing so. It is little wonder then that parents do not teach self-management or self-control to their child when they think there is only one authority relationship.

Parents need to teach the child from **three years of age** on the **five authority relationships** so that the child will interact responsibly with all human beings. This is how the conflict over "Who's Boss?" is resolved and harmonious relationships are maintained.

Chapter 2

Conflicts of Authority

Repeatable Activities

Following are some of the repeatable activities that frustrate parents.

> Pick up your clothes.
> Please don't talk with your mouth full.
> Sit still.
> Do not interrupt while mother is talking.

Parents who constantly remind their children to do repeatable activities do not know how to teach self-management. Many parents suffer from anxiety, become emotionally upset, lose their temper, and wind up yelling at their children. These are the feelings of helplessness and cries for help from parents. Their cries for help go something like this:

"Why doesn't my child obey me? What am I doing wrong? I have become a nag. I only tell my child what is good for him. He just won't listen. What can I do to correct this?"

These are the reports Dr, Wise receives from mothers who come into his office seeking help. Until mothers learn to use the five keys to self-management, the conflicts of authority between parent and child will continue.

Example: A Misunderstanding Of Authority

One day a twenty-six-year-old mother, named Mrs. Johnson, walked into Dr. Wise's office because her seven-year-old daughter, named Susie, was out of control. She lost control over her daughter by repeating instructions and expecting compliance to happen naturally, thereby unintentionally supporting Susie's refusal to boss herself. Both mother and child had a serious misunderstanding of authority relationships which had to be corrected.

Mrs. Johnson, unknowingly, taught Susie to be disobedient. She did not teach her to boss herself, to do daily **repeatable activities** on the basis of rules and routines. Susie also did not know the difference between parental authority and Susie's personal authority. She did not know that mother exercised three kinds of authority: **personal**, **parental**, and **impersonal**. These are three of the five keys to self-management.

The day Mrs. Johnson came in to see Dr. Wise, he could tell by the tone of her voice that she was very upset. Her story went something like this:

"Dr. Wise, I am very depressed and heartbroken about my little Susie. She is very demanding and expects her father and me to jump at her every command. But when we ask her to do something, she just ignores us or simply tells us she is too busy. She is bossy, disobedient, and uncontrollable. I am at my wits end trying to deal with her. I am almost ashamed to say she is my daughter. Can you help my little Susie, Doctor?"

"Of course I can, Mrs. Johnson. Exactly how is Susie disobedient to you and your husband?"

"Susie has terrible table manners. She never sits still long enough to finish a meal. She gets up in the middle of dinner to get a toy or something to amuse herself. She has been doing this ever since she was able to walk. As a result, she is a bad eater and is constantly distracting herself. She spoils the dinner hour for my husband and me by always calling attention to herself and constantly interrupting our conversations.

"At first, when Susie was a toddler, my husband and I thought she was cute and indulged her with her demands. We just laughed and thought her to be very smart. She is older now, and it is getting worse. We can't make her sit still at the table. She is constantly complaining about her food. She can't ever decide what she wants to eat. She says, 'This is no good. That tastes bad, or that tastes terrible.' I cannot please her no matter how much I try. Besides having bad table manners, Susie never puts anything away. She pulls out all of her toys, plus all of my things and her father's."

Dr. Wise questioned. "What do you mean by your things and her father's?"

"Susie will go into my drawers without permission. She takes out my perfume and puts it on. One time I found her pouring my best perfume down the toilet. Another time I found her taking out her father's jewelry (tie clips and cuff links). When I told her to put them back, she just dropped them on the floor and refused to do it. She just walked away. With this I spanked her and sent her to her room. This did no good, for the next day she was at it again. Whatever am I going to do with this child, Doctor?"

Dr. Wise: "Mrs Johnson, you and Susie are having authority conflicts, but you came to the right place to correct your difficulties."

Bossing Yourself

Dr. Wise sat back in his chair and thought for a moment, deciding which of Mrs. Johnson's problems to correct first — the problem with her or with Susie. He decided to teach Mrs. Johnson first.

"Mrs Johnson, have you tried to teach Susie to boss herself?"

"Boss herself? What do you mean by 'boss herself'?"

"Bossing oneself is another word for self-control. To ask a child if she can boss herself has proven to be a more understandable phrase for a child, than the phrase 'can you self-control yourself'. Susie can understand that she can tell herself what to do. She can boss herself. She does not need to be repeatedly told by you what to do. You can give her a rule for a repeatable activity. Then, you must expect her to boss herself with a rule or routine. This will relieve you from bossing her. What we want Susie to understand, at her age, is that she can boss herself. A parent does not need to control her constantly while she is doing repeatable activities."

"Dr. Wise, what do you mean by 'repeatable activities'?"

"Repeatable activities are activities one must do every day; such as — putting away clothes, brushing teeth, combing hair, picking up toys or sitting still at the dinner table. Do you see that these are activities which are repeated daily?"

Conflicts of Authority

"Yes Doctor, I do now that you explained it that way, I can see that Susie does refuse to do repeatable activities on a daily basis. So to avoid a useless conflict, I usually dress her in the morning, put away her toys in the evening, brush and comb her hair, accept her bad manners at dinner, etc. I have just not been able to get her to do these repeatable activities without forcing her."

"Because you have not made her responsible for any of her activities, she will hold on to baby habits. Do you see how you are not training Susie out of her infantile behavior?"

"But Susie will not listen to me, Doctor."

"That is not true. Susie usually hears your instructions, but she knows that she doesn't have to obey until you threaten to hurt her."

Mechanical Repeatable Activities

There are two types of repeatable activities: **mechanical** and **social**. Everyone uses repeatable activities daily. Mechanical activities, such as brushing teeth, using the toilet, getting dressed and undressed, putting away toys are some of the activities that parents must teach the child when he reaches a certain level of maturity. But until the child reaches that stage of maturity, a parent guides the child through mechanical steps he eventually will follow by himself. If the parent is not consistent, then the child will also not be consistent.

Social Repeatable Activities

The same is true for social repeatable activities, such as using proper courtesies like: please, thank you, excuse me, good morning, you're welcome, have a nice day, etc.

However, social repeatable activities begin with the infant. The parent talks to the infant, not ever expecting him to answer, but just getting the infant used to the sound of words and smiling and saying cute, funny things; such as, "You beautiful baby, smile for mother, see da da." The parents are making a rapport with their child. Of course, the child will not speak until he reaches a certain level of maturity.

When baby starts to grasp things and hands objects to mother, this is mother's opportunity to start training her child in courtesies, by saying, "Thank you. You're welcome."

By mother using repeatable social courtesies and being consistent, she is creating a framework for her child to follow.

Dr. Wise explained to Mrs. Johnson that by using repeatable mechanical activities and social phrases daily from infancy through the toddler stage, a parent lays down the foundation for her child to become courteous.

"But, you Mrs. Johnson had no idea that this is what you were suppose to do with Susie, so you never shifted the authority from you to Susie."

"Shift? How do you make this shift? Doctor."

Shifting Authority
Step No. 1
"The first step is to teach Susie that you will repeat instructions only twice. Tell her that when she was two- and three-years-old, it was necessary to repeat instructions. Explain to her that you want her to let go of baby habits.

"If you remember, Mrs. Johnson, at two and three Susie had a limited understanding of words. She was unable, at times, to coordinate or understand bodily movements. You had to repeat your instructions and be responsible for her actions. Susie is now seven. She can be responsible for repeatable activities. She now has a larger vocabulary and can regulate herself. Her coordination has improved to the extent that you can trust her to do many things without falling, breaking things, or hurting herself.

"Mrs. Johnson, during this time you developed a habit of repeating yourself many times when Susie was in the toddler stage. Susie got into the habit of expecting you to repeat yourself many times. You made yourself totally responsible for her actions when she was capable of doing things for herself.

"As Susie grew older, she became increasingly capable of being responsible for her own activities, but you did not realize that you needed to shift the responsibility of various activities from you to her. You continued Susie in her baby dependency habits.

"Now you must break Susie's total dependency on you by telling her something like this: 'Susie, I will tell you **once** to pick up your clothes. If I say this is the **second** time, I expect you to do what needs to be done. I don't want to hear any alibis or excuses or you will go to your room to think about it.'

"By telling her this, you will stop her baby habits and stop her from ignoring your instructions, as you now have her attention. She will come to know from experience that you will not nag or repeat yourself. She will know when you give her the cue words, 'This is the second time,' you expect a prompt response from her or she will go to her room.

"She must also understand that there will be no more emotional temper tantrums to avoid doing what is requested. You will also no longer rely on emotional distress to control her.

"If you find yourself getting emotionally upset, stop and collect your thoughts. After all, Susie has had seven years to develop her ability to trigger you into an emotionally agitated state. This is when you must learn self-control in order to use parental authority properly."

Step No. 2

"Ask Susie, 'Can you boss yourself?'

"When you say this, you are shifting the responsibility to Susie. Although she may not always know what you are doing, the important idea is that you know what you are doing — shifting the responsibility to Susie.

"When you ask her, 'Can you boss yourself?' Susie can accept this idea as it has been established that a child can understand the idea of bossing.

"Susie will answer, 'I can boss myself.'

"If you make it a fun activity for her, she may even answer with pride that she can boss herself. Tell her this is an important adult habit she is acquiring.

"When presented properly, Susie will have the incentive to feel like a big girl and will gladly accept the idea of bossing herself. With this, you have made the shift from parental authority to impersonal authority. It is important for Susie to realize that in order to boss herself effectively, she must not depend upon an external source to continually motivate her.

"She must know that there will be no third request, but a consequence for not bossing herself. The acts of disobedi ence and irresponsibility must stop. She must learn to take your suggestions seriously. A habit of obedience must be established."

Step No. 3

"The third step is to teach Susie that there are rules and routines for repeatable activities. Rules and routines help to prevent a parent, teacher, or adult from having to boss a child. They provide a means for Susie to boss herself."

"Rules and routines? But she is too young to obey rules and routines, isn't she?" Mrs. Johnson looking at me rather quizzically.

I could see from our conversation that Mrs. Johnson knew very little about authority relationships. She, like many parents, believed only one authority relationship (parental authority) existed. The concept of more than one authority relationship was a totally new idea. Knowing this to be true from over the many years in practice, I developed the concept of the five authority relationships.

Mrs. Johnson thought, as do many mothers, that a child naturally learned to obey at some future date. She expected Susie, on the basis of reason, to eventually acquire repeatable activities. But some children would rather remain dependent to get out of work or to get out of taking care of themselves.

Like all mothers, Mrs. Johnson had seen Susie go through physical stages and had seen the related changes in social behavior. She thought being taken care of was one of the stages Susie would grow out of. She didn't know that this was one of the many infantile habits and ways of thinking that a child tries to maintain. She didn't know she had to train her daughter out of being dependent.

Babies and children grow out of one physical stage into another. This, however, does not necessarily apply to social development and certainly not to self-management.

Mrs. Johnson and Susie have been following rules and routines since the day Susie was born. Neither one recognized that this was what they were doing. Everyone uses the five authority relationships whether they know it or not. Now my job was to explain the five authority relationships to Mrs. Johnson so that she understands when to use them and how to use rules and routines to shift authority from her to Susie.

"Did you know, Mrs. Johnson, that Susie has been obeying rules, although no one told her what a rule was or what rule she was obeying."

"No I didn't."

"When you told Susie at two- and three-years-old to look to the left and then to the right to see if there were any cars coming in either direction before crossing the street, she was learning a rule. When you told her to cross the street at the intersection and only to cross when the light turned green, that was another rule. When you told her not to talk at the table with her mouth full of food, that was also a rule. When she learned to put on her underclothes, dress, socks, and shoes before eating breakfast, she was learning a dress routine. Even as an infant, there were eating and diaper routines. Rules and routines are used with the five authority relationships that every child must learn."

"Doctor, I am now beginning to feel confident that my husband and I will be able to help Susie. First, though, please tell me about the five authority relationships."

Chapter 3

The Five Authority Relationships

Self -Management

The foundation of successful human relations rests on the five authority relationships (the framework of self-management). The future of any person is determined between the ages of four to six. I am fairly certain that many mothers and fathers are not aware of how important these two years are in the life of a child.

As a psychologist, I have spent many years in my office listening to parents and their children telling me their problems. I found that a few adults had superior parents. All other adults were reared either by first-time or amateur parents. The superior parents passed on what they learned from their parents to their children.

Over the years I developed the five authority relationships in self-management. You will not find them written in any other book, as these concepts have been successfully used in my office over and over again when talking with parents who have had problems similar to Mrs. Johnson's. Many of these concepts are centuries old and have been tried and proven to be successful time and time again.

The following week Mrs. Johnson came in to see me, and I introduced her to the five authority relationships.

Personal Relationships

"**Bossing others, bossing yourself,** and **being bossed by others.** " I paused for Mrs. Johnson to grasp these three relationships.

"But that is only three relationships," she remarked."

"That's right." These are the three personal relationships every baby practices prior to the age of four. In fact, every human being, whether they know it or not, practice using these three relationships throughout their lifetime.

A parent will tell a child, "You are too bossy." Or a child will say to another child or an adult, "You can't boss me." So you see by these remarks children and parents are aware of these relationships, but if not trained to recognize and use them, they more than likely will have a hit-or-miss experience.

A parent needs to teach these three relationships to a child during ages three to six so that the child will know how to use them properly as he matures.

The other two relationships are external to the child, which are learned after the age of four. These two relationships can only be explained after a child can speak enough words and understand social relationships. They are **delegated authority and impersonal authority."**

Using The Bossing Relationships

"But how do the five authority relationships work? I'm confused. I never heard of or knew that there were five authority relationships until today, Dr. Wise. Please explain them to me."

"Of course I will. You see, I must train you to use the five authority relationships and to use them with Susie. When you go home today, there are three concepts you can immediately implant into Susie's mind.

First, do not repeat yourself more than twice.
Second, start labeling the authority relationships.
Third, gradually change infantile thinking and habits

into a considerate way of thinking, along with learning acceptable habits for her age.

"Susie needs to acquire some thinking tools if she is to let go of her infantile habits. She must have a reason for letting go of old secure ways, which you will supply for her.

"You may not think Susie's demanding and acting like an infant is her security blanket, but it is. She wants to act like an adult and does so, in certain ways, such as dressing up like mother, wanting to wear lipstick, etc. She will have to be trained out of her infantile ways first if she is to become a mature adult.

"The fact is, you have reinforced her infantile ways by repeating your instructions over and over, thus failing to dethrone her. You continued her clinging to the demanding "little queen" role. Monarchs prior to the Magna Carta did not care most of the time about their subjects' feelings or rights. They did what they wanted to do. This is the way of all babies, including Susie — they are selfish, inconsiderate, and hostile if they don't get their way. You added to her problems because you thought she would mature and develop fair attitudes of relating to other people on her own."

Mrs. Johnson replies, "I am beginning to see my misunderstandings as a parent. I have been naive in raising Susie. Now I can see I did not talk to Susie like she was a changing individual. I have been looking at her as my baby. What a fool I have been. I was the one who didn't change my behavior when Susie started to change hers. My husband and I must be as frustrating to Susie as she is to us."

"That's right, Mrs. Johnson. The big difference is that you and your husband can seek help to resolve difficulties.

Susie doesn't know how to seek help. Until she can boss herself, she will remain helpless. Unless you and your husband help her to apply the authority relationships, Susie will grow up physically, but will remain a small child in many of her relationships. **Authority relationships are the framework to self-management."**

Effective Bossing Interactions

"Okay, Dr. Wise, I understand what **bossing**, **being bossed** and **bossing another** means when used separately, but how do the three relationships work together."

"Well, these relationships are in effect whenever individuals interact with each other. Let's take a family situation and see how the three authority relationships work.

It is morning:

Mother gets up, puts the coffee on (bosses herself).

Mother awakens hubby. (bosses another).

Mother continues her routine by awakening the children (children being bossed)."

"Now I see what you mean, Dr. Wise. It is true we do use the authority relationships every morning at our house. It does help to label them. I now know how they interact with each other. They are easy to understand once you know what to look for."

"This is true, Mrs. Johnson."

The Five Authority Relationships

When a child is too small, mother dresses him, or she has an older child help. But this does not mean mother is not bossing the younger child, preparing him for the day when he will dress himself. Mother watches the child to see if he is ready to manage himself. She may start by handing him his socks. When he can do this, she hands him his pants and then his shirt. She may, at first, have to button the shirt and tie his shoes — but that's okay. At this point, the youngster has made the transition from being dressed to dressing himself. The responsibility is being shifted. He is giving up baby habits of having someone else completely dress him. The trick is for mother to recognize when the child is ready to take on a new responsibility.

This action is called the principle of independence — when a child is ready to take care of himself, the parent expects him to do so. It is a part of bossing oneself, or executing self-management.

"What if the child refuses to become independent? Susie has refused to do anything for herself, Doctor."

The Art Of Distraction

"Mrs. Johnson, you have not mastered the art of distraction. If you distract Susie with the new idea of bossing herself and make it sound like fun, then she may be excited enough to give up her baby habits. You must make growing and developing an exciting experience. Susie should look forward each day to increasing her skills in self-management.

"Don't make remarks about how terrible it is to be an adult and wish you were a child again. Many adults discourage children from wanting to grow up this way.

"When Susie comes to my office, I can reinforce and help her to understand the three keys to self-management. By the time you and Susie have had enough appointments, she will have fun bossing herself. You will no longer have to worry whether she is able to manage herself."

Impersonal & Delegated Authority

"Dr. Wise, I can now understanding the three authority relationships. Can you tell me what delegated and impersonal authority mean?"

"Certainly. The community has various authority persons like the teacher, the policeman, the senator, the clergyman to whom have been given authority to represent and control other people. They have what is called delegated authority.

"I guess you can say parents have natural authority. Parental authority is also delegated authority as well. Parents exercise both personal and parental authority. Sometimes a parent controls a child with personal authority and at other times with parental authority."

"Dr. Wise, doesn't everybody have personal authority?"

"Yes. Anytime one bosses another person, that is personal authority."

Difference - Personal & Parental Authority

When a child is old enough to be left at home and you give him a choice to go with you or to stay at home, this is personal authority. Personal authority involves a choice.

When a child has no choice, this is parental authority.

The Five Authority Relationships

A child usually knows that he can request anything, but that you have the parental authority to say, "yes" or "no."

"Mrs. Johnson, let's take a family situation such as the dinner hour. You ask your husband to pass the butter. Are you not bossing him by asking him to do something?

"Yes."

"And when he passes you the butter, is he not allowing you to boss him?"

"Yes."

"Isn't this the way we communicate with one another by using our personal authority?"

"Yes. I can see that now, Dr. Wise."

"Can you also see that personal authority is constantly shifting from one person to another?"

"Yes, I can. But now Dr, Wise, can you tell me how impersonal authority is used?"

"This is controlled by rules, routines, laws, and policies. This gives a person the opportunity to control himself and not to be controlled by authority persons. This is also a way of saving money. When the policeman who was directing traffic at the intersection was replaced by the red, amber, and green lights, millions of dollars were saved. The efficiency of impersonal authority can be demonstrated by the intersection lights and traffic signs.

"The metal container with green, amber and red lights are termed impersonal authority. There is no person there with delegated authority to direct traffic. Just the lights changing colors tell the driver or pedestrian what to do. The effectiveness of the system depends upon the person being able and willing to boss himself. All persons are treated equally as long as they boss themselves.

"When the policeman is directing traffic, he uses both personal authority and delegated authority.

"Another example of impersonal authority is the lines in a parking lot, telling a driver where to park the car. There are all the traffic signs on the freeway also telling a motorist what to do."

"Thank you, Doctor. I now understand impersonal and delegated authority."

"Once you get Susie to understand that you are not going to repeat instructions, she will begin to manage herself according to her age, and not according to infantile behavior."

Using Repeatable Activities

"Pick a repeatable activity to start training Susie how to boss herself."

"Which one should we pick? Doctor."

"Oh, let's start with meal times," Dr. Wise suggested.

"That's fine with me. Anything to bring peace to the dinner table."

"When you call Susie to the table, does she come?"

"No. Not usually."

The Five Authority Relationships

"Well, before the next meal time, sit down and have a talk with her. Ask her if she would like to have some fun bossing herself. She should agree, but if she doesn't, do not let that bother you. Just go about explaining to her the sequences and routines relating to dinner to teach Susie the priorities and sequences of the dinner hour.

"First, ask her if she sits in a highchair at dinner time? The answer you get may be, 'No. I am a big girl, now.'

"Then, tell her since she is no longer a baby who must be carried to the highchair that, when you call her to dinner, you expect her to stop what she is doing and come immediately. A baby must wait for someone to carry her, but a big girl seats herself when called to dinner.

"Now is the time to make this an exciting event for Susie. You will be, in effect, introducing her to etiquette. **Etiquette consists of courtesies and manners by using a simple rule or routine.**

"After everyone is seated, ask Susie what is the 'next priority'? Susie may answer, 'I don't know, Mommy.'

"You tell her that a 'priority' is a new word for her, and a 'next priority' means what happens after coming to the table.

"For example: we all take our places, greet one another, perhaps say a prayer, and then pass or serve the food. After each sequence of the meal, keep asking her for the next priority until she understands the sequence followed at meal time. At the conclusion of the meal, ask her to explain why you have gone through the dinner routine. She may not have a clue, but she will think about what you have said.

"Then say something to this effect: **Etiquette and table manners are to teach self-management** at dinner so that neither your father nor I will have to boss you. You can now

27

boss yourself. This is also to teach you how to boss others. Etiquette is following rules to be used at the dinner table. You are now old enough to start learning about table manners. These are the same rules that adults use. This will make you feel grown up and will let all of us have a pleasant feeling towards one another. This is what etiquette relationships are for.

"I know you have never thought about any of this before, Mrs. Johnson, but keep in mind that this little routine will get Susie thinking, and it doesn't have to be elaborate or perfectly thought out. Do you think you can teach Susie these simple **principles of etiquette**?"

"Yes, Doctor. I am excited to see how Susie will respond to bossing herself at dinner time."

"This is just the beginning to get Susie to boss herself at meal times. As for the other activities, we will work together on those, too, week by week. Let's just take a few steps at a time. The **key to success** in teaching self-management to Susie **is consistency**. At first, you will have to initiate table manners, until she begins to use them without prompting her. Now, it is time for Susie to visit me so I can reinforce your efforts in teaching her to boss herself at home."

Chapter 4

Teaching Authority Relationships

Bossing Yourself

A few days later Susie came in to see me for her first appointment. I asked her, "Susie, are you and your Mother having difficulties getting along with each other?"

"What do you mean, Dr. Wise?"

"Well, Susie, are you and your Mother always fighting about one thing or another? Does your Mother become upset with you?"

"Yes," she replied.

"Would you like to make your Mother feel better and not become angry with you?"

"Yes."

"I can help you make your Mother feel better and you can have a lot more fun with her. Would you like that, Susie?"

"Oh yes, I would like that, Doctor," she replied.

"Okay, Susie, let's play a question and answer game. I will ask you the questions and you give me the answers. I promise you that by the time we finish this little game you will be a lot happier and know what to do in many situations to make your Mom happy." Susie liked the idea of playing a question game and was willing to make her mother happy. This told me that Susie could be a cooperative child when given explanations.

"Susie," I said, "When your Mother asks you to put away your clothes, do you do it?"

"No."

"Why not?" I asked.

"Oh, I mean to put them away."

"But you usually don't."

"Oh, I know Mom will forget about it."

"Are you not afraid of being punished for not doing what you are told to do?"

"No. All Mother does is just talk. I pretend to listen and sometimes if I feel like it, I will pick up my clothes. If I don't feel like it, I do not pick up my clothes."

I said to Susie, "Can you boss yourself?"

Susie looked curiously at me and asked, "What do you mean, boss yourself?"

"Bossing yourself means, you tell yourself what to do and you do it," I told her.

"Oh yes, I can boss myself. That's easy to do, Doctor," she said proudly, all smiles. Then she frowned and asked, "But why should I boss myself?"

Teaching Authority Relationship

Being Bossed

"If you boss yourself, you will not have to **be bossed** by your parents. You will feel better about being able to control yourself. Do you like being bossed by your Mother?"

"No."

"There is also another way to keep yourself from being bossed."

"How, Dr. Wise?"

"Well, you first have to be given a set of rules and routines to follow. Can you tell me who gives you rules and routines to follow?"

"Oh, yes, Mother does."

"Can you tell me what rules your Mother gives you to follow at the dinner table?"

Well, apparently Mrs. Johnson had done an excellent job on instructing Susie on how to behave at the dinner table. Susie gave me a step-by-step description that she followed at meal times. However, she still was not doing everything that was expected of her. But, Susie had a good start — she now knew what rules and routines to follow for dinner. Eventually, she will begin to follow routines more and more at dinner time as she becomes used to using the three authority relationships. She will also find out that it is more fun to boss herself than to have someone else boss her.

"Susie," I asked, "did your Mother tell you that you were to sit still and not get up while everyone was eating? That the only way you were allowed to leave the dinner table was by saying, 'May I please be excused'?"

31

"Oh, yes! I remember Mother did tell me that."

"Mother tells me that you still are getting up and down while eating your meal. Are you doing a good job of bossing yourself when you do that, Susie?"

"No. I guess I am not, Dr. Wise."

"Did Mother also tell you that you were not to interrupt Daddy and her while they were talking?"

"Yes, I guess she did."

"What did she tell you about interrupting? Can you tell me, Susie?"

"I forgot, Doctor."

"Didn't she tell you that if you had something to say, you were to say, 'Excuse me, Mother, I would like to tell you something,' and wait until she gives you permission to speak?"

"No, Doctor, Mother did not tell me that."

Well, I had my answer. Mother and Susie had a good start. It would take many therapy sessions to get both of them to understand how to use self-management effectively.

There are many habits to be learned associated with authority relationships. Since Mrs. Johnson has started a little late in shifting the responsibility from parent to child, she will have to catch up gradually teaching Susie the tricks of bossing others, being bossed, and bossing herself. Mrs. Johnson had many lessons to learn about how to make the shift of responsibility from parent to child and other personal management relationships.

Teaching Authority Relationship

Susie, however, was beginning to understand and co-operate with her mother. I continued to ask her questions to reinforce Mrs. Johnson's efforts in teaching Susie self-management.

Bossing Others
"Can you boss another person, Susie?"

"What do you mean, Dr. Wise?"

"Can you ask, or tell, another person to do something?"

"When you tell me that way, I know what you mean. Yes. I can tell my Daddy what to do, and he does it every time," she said proudly, giggling.

"Susie, did you know that there are three ways of bossing?"

"No. I did not know that, Dr. Wise."

"Didn't your Mother tell you about the three ways of bossing?"

"I guess she did, but I only remember her telling me about bossing myself."

This is why I review the three relationships with children as parents sometimes do not thoroughly explain the authority relationships to their children.

"**First, bossing yourself:** Susie, I know you know how to do that. You told me you did."

"Yes, Dr. Wise. I can boss myself."

33

"**Second**, **being bossed** is having someone else boss you. Like Mother asking you to pick up your clothes."

"Oh, yes. Now I remember, Mother did tell me that she can boss me to pick up my clothes and that she would only tell me twice."

"Very good, Susie. Can you remember what else your Mother said if you didn't obey her?"

"Yes, Doctor, she would send me to my room to think about it."

"Excellent! Susie. You named for me the first and the second authority relationships. Now, tell me the **Third** authority relationship, bossing others. Do you remember it? Think real hard because you told it to me a while ago."

Susie sat there trying to remember something she said a while back. Then her eyes lit up, and she blurted out with pride in her voice, "Yes, I remember, I can boss my Daddy."

"Yes, Susie, that is right, and that is called, bossing others, or bossing another person like your mom, dad, or a friend. These are the **three personal authority relationships** I want you to use from now on. Do you think you will have fun using them?"

"Oh, Yes, Dr. Wise. I can boss myself. I can boss my Daddy and Mother. Mother can boss me, too."

"So Susie, let us have fun using the three personal bossing relationships."

Teaching Authority Relationship

For the rest of the hour, Susie and I had fun using the three personal relationships until I thought she had a fair idea of how to use them.

Impersonal & Delegated Authority

At Susie's next appointment, I introduced her to the last two authority relationships. This is how our session began.

"Susie, there are two more special authority relationships I want you to know about. They are **delegated authority and impersonal authority.**

Delegated authority is being bossed by authority persons such as teachers, policemen, babysitters, etc.

Impersonal authority is being bossed by rules and routines, like at the dinner table."

I knew Susie didn't understand what I had just said about delegated and impersonal authority, so I decided to give her some examples of what I was talking about.

"Let's see how these authority relationships work in a baseball game. Do you know how to play baseball, Susie?"

"Oh yes, Dr. Wise. I play baseball with my Daddy."

"Okay! When you are the batter in a baseball game are you being bossed?"

"No," answered Susie.

"Yes you are. The pitcher is bossing you and if there is an umpire, he is there to boss everyone on the infield and outfield. The umpire exercises delegated authority.

Are you bossing yourself at bat, Susie?

She paused to think a moment. "Yes, I have to hit the ball and get myself to first base. Then, when the next hitter bosses himself to hit the ball, I must again boss myself and run as fast as I can to second base and third base and maybe home plate."

"Very good, Susie. Now can you tell me when you are bossing others?"

She thought a moment and said, "When I holler at Margie to get a player out, I say, 'Throw it here, Margie! Throw it here!' That is bossing my friend. I tell her to throw the ball to me."

"That's right, Susie. You've got the idea. You must practice being bossed and bossing yourself in order to be good at it. Then you will have a more enjoyable experience relating to family and friends. Susie, tell me who is the parent — you or your Mother?"

"That is easy — Mother is."

"When you don't do what you are asked to do, you are keeping your Mother from being the parent. Did you know that?"

"No, I did not, Dr. Wise."

"You become the parent and then your Mother gets angry with you. Can you tell me why she gets angry at you?"

"Because I do not do what she tells me to do."

"That is partially true, Susie. She is also getting angry at you because you can't boss yourself and you will not let her be the parent. Until you can boss yourself, you are not managing yourself very well. You are not being a big girl. You are not playing fair. When you do not boss yourself, you are holding on to your baby habits. Mother is training you to be a big girl and a self-manager. Do you want to be a self-manager?"

"Oh, yes, Dr. Wise," she promptly replied.

"That's very good, Susie. Did you know you were coming here to get training in self-management?"

"No. I thought I was coming to see you because Mother was always angry at me."

"Do you like the idea that I am going to teach you how to boss yourself?"

"Oh, yes. This is fun. I like to tell myself what to do. I never thought about doing that before. I like to boss myself. I like to boss others. And now I like others to boss me. It is a super game. I know why others must boss me too," she smiled happily.

"It's a give and take relationship, isn't it Susie?"

"I guess so."

"Did you know that this is what being grown up is all about?"

"No, but it sounds like fun."

"That's right, Susie. Self-management is a word for controlling your repeatable activities; such as doing homework, playing at recess time or gym periods, taking care of your room, and doing chores at home. Anything you do must be controlled by you. Controlling your activities and yourself is called self-management.

Now that you are aware of the five keys to self-management, you will begin to use them more often," I told her.

Susie came to see me twice a week for two months before Mrs. Johnson and her husband became a winner in the struggle with their daughter. Susie learned to use the five keys to self-management very well, and we found that once she got started, she became a very cooperative child.

Reason and consideration had not been effective in controlling Susie's actions because her mother had not taught her to obey on the first or second instruction. Susie was too often controlled by her feelings and her lack of consideration. Susie's self-control was like that of a three-year-old child when she refused to boss herself and was not willing to be obedient to authority persons.

Mrs. Johnson found out that making herself unhappy did not teach Susie self-management. Susie refused to be obedient with no regard for anyone's feelings. Not even reason worked until Mrs. Johnson took Susie to my office to learn the five keys to self-management.

While Mrs. Johnson was in my office, I also taught her how to be a **habit trainer**.

PART II - THE HABIT TRAINER

Chapter 5

Habit Trainers

A System Of Habits

No one can live without habits. Human beings are creatures of habit. Everyone acquires habits usually without being aware of it, except to complain about a bad habit. Habits are just taken for granted by everyone.

A habit is frequently thought of as something bad, rather than as something desirable. A habit can be thought of as interfering with a person's freedom. Actually, though, habits give a person freedom.

Coaches and music teachers are very aware of habit training. They create a system of habits to be learned by their athletes or students. They insist that a system of habits be practiced until the habits can be performed without thinking.

Mothers do not wake up in the morning, like coaches or teachers, wondering about a system of habits they are going to teach their baby or child for the day. But, every mother does teach her child an act or phase of self-management; such as dressing, washing hands and face, brushing teeth, etc.

For every act of self-management there is a system of habits to be learned. Before a child can play a tune on the piano, there are many habits to be acquired.

In order to teach and learn the acts of self-management, both parent and child need to use the five authority relationships.

The system of habits and authority relationships are interlaced like a shoe string in the eyelets of a boot.

Acts Of Self-Management

No act of self-management, such as ice skating, dancing, playing the piano, or toilet habits, can be effective without intertwining habits with authority relationships.

It is the steady pressure of parental authority that helps a child acquire the thousands of necessary habits needed for hundreds of acts in self-management.

If a parent does not connect the five authority relationships with habits while helping a child learn an act of self-management, the child may become an aggravation to parents and other people as well.

Susie was an aggravation until she knew how to use authority relationships. She then acquired the habits necessary to make dinner a pleasant time for the family.

As I tell you about Joan, a young mother expecting her first baby in seven months, you will have a better understanding of habit training. As with so many first-time mothers, Joan did not know about the autonomic system, maturational patterning, authority relationships, subconscious and conscious minds, or systems of habits. To be a superior habit trainer she had to know these concepts. Even without knowing the labels for them, Joan would still unknowingly use these concepts to train her child.

Joan came into my office asking questions about training her baby. She was expressing both her confidence and her fears as a new expectant parent will do.

"Dr. Wise, I know this is going to sound silly, but there is something bothering me," Joan began with a look of helplessness on her face.

"Don't be concerned with whether you sound silly, Joan. If something is bothering you, say it. Then, I can help you by explaining how to get rid of your fears. Hopefully, our discussions will lead to secure feelings. That is what I'm here for," I reassured her.

"Okay, I will tell you my feelings. Babies just born are so fragile, and I'm afraid of not being able to handle my child. What if I accidentally knock off his belly button tie while washing him? How will I know what to do when he cries when I have already fed and burped him? Oh, Doctor, I have so many questions to ask about raising my baby."

"What do you and your husband want — a boy or a girl?" I questioned.

"We would like a boy. We already have a name for him, David," she proudly told me.

I smiled and thought seriously for a moment and then told her, "Joan, you won't knock off your baby's belly tie. Every mother is puzzled and concerned about how to physically manage her child. She is also concerned about how to train the child to manage himself, to do the many things that a child must do to become an effective human being.

"Dr. Wise, how do I train my child to sit up, to walk, to talk, and to obey? Obeying — that's the one thing that really has me puzzled. How do you get a child to do what needs to be done? How does a parent manage a child?"

"Joan, I will answer all your questions and many more now and in future sessions. I will teach you how to manage your child, but more importantly what you really want to do is to teach your child how to manage himself rather than to be managed by you. Self-management is the word you are looking for."

Surprised, Joan said, "Self-management? What's that? What does that have to do with a newborn?"

As Joan was a new client, I knew from past experiences that I had to start from the beginning as I didn't know how much she knew about having a baby and rearing him.

"Joan, I will explain more thoroughly how the **five authority relationships, systems of habits, and acts of self-management interrelate.** This will help you rear your child to manage himself. Joan, parents are habit trainers. My job now is to teach you to be a habit trainer. The first step for you to realize is that baby from inception bosses himself. The first authority relationship you need to be aware of is that your baby is now bossing himself through the autonomic system. After birth, you, as a parent, will teach him **acts of self-management** so that he can boss himself. You then will not have to boss him too often. As he acquires more and more s**ystems of habits**, which are necessary for bossing himself, your fears and anxieties will diminish. When your baby develops and masters many acts of self-management, he will eventually boss himself. To be able to boss himself, he will need to learn a lot of system of habits, and you, Joan, will teach him these habits one at a time."

The Autonomic System

"You mean my baby is bossing himself now?"

"Yes, that's what your baby is doing at this very moment."

"Oh, Doctor, are you joshing?" Joan questioned.

"No, I am not. I am serious. Self-management is natural. It begins the moment a baby is conceived. For weeks and months the unborn baby experiences self-management.

Habit Trainers

"Baby swims in his own exclusive pool with no one to boss him or comfort him. He exercises his rapidly growing body by swimming. Eventually mother feels baby kicking or poking her when he tries to exercise his legs and arms in his pool, which becomes progressively smaller.

"Baby is also learning to hear and to feel vibrations from the outside environment. Some scientists think that babies can hear soundwaves. Baby's home is dark, but he doesn't care as he doesn't know what light is yet.

"By the time baby's pool shrinks to the point that it becomes necessary for him to leave for the outside environment, he has already faced many drastic bodily changes on his own within the amniotic sac. In this very restricted and protected environment, baby has already learned to manage himself."

"You mean all this is happening inside me now? I never thought about my baby managing himself at this very moment. 'Well, David,' Joan said as she patted her stomach, 'I hope you enjoy your swim and your lunch.'

"How do I teach my baby to manage or boss himself when he arrives? What are the other four authority relationships and when do I use them? Tell me, what do habits have to do with self-management, Doctor?"

"Whoa, one question at a time, Joan. For the first ninety days there is not much to do in the way of training the newborn infant except to feed, diaper, and give him good physical care and affection. Prior to birth, the infant is under the control of the autonomic system which manages him very well. After the infant is born, his eating,

43

sleeping, breathing, defecating, urinating is still under the control of the autonomic system."

"So after ninety days, will I still be feeding him and letting the autonomic system take care of him? When does the autonomic system give me a chance?" asked Joan.

"The autonomic system, a part of the subconscious mind, is mainly in control until the infant begins to sit up. Then you get your chance to habit train him — thanks to the conscious mind gradually taking over."

Conscious & Subconscious Minds

"Conscious and subconscious minds — what does this have to do with training my child, Dr. Wise?"

"We can think of the brain as being divided into a conscious mind and a subconscious mind. This is a very simple and useful explanation, particularly when we think and talk about training.

"The child's conscious mind decides whether to accept or reject a habit. Once the conscious decision has been made to accept a habit, the child can then repeat the habit until the habit is recorded in the subconscious mind. Then the habit becomes automatic. At that point you are successful as a habit trainer because you no longer have to boss your child for that habit. He can boss himself.

"Baby's self-management increases with every system of habit and acts he acquires. This is why it is important that you direct his learning of habits.

"During the first weeks, however, the subconscious mind is definitely in control. Gradually the conscious mind takes over the management but, until it does, you really can do little to train him."

Habit Trainers

Baby Habit Trains Himself

Joan sat very still listening to how her baby will habit train himself. I explained, "One of the visible signs of conscious self-management can be seen as baby clasps his chubby hands around an object and places it in his mouth. Baby consciously does this. It may be out of curiosity or without understanding why. Baby likes to grab anything he can reach so that he can put it in his mouth to taste. Sooner or later he puts something into his mouth that doesn't taste good. He quickly learns to spit it out, generally making a funny face when doing this. This is probably the beginning of **taste discrimination**.

"When baby is ready, he takes an important step in consciously learning a habit by self-observation. He first watches objects, other persons, and himself. When he accidentally makes a movement he likes, he again, perhaps by accident, makes that movement and repeats it again and again until it becomes a meaningful action to him. At the moment the movement becomes meaningful, baby acquires the self-learned habit for himself.

"During the first weeks, when you are taking care of your baby you will see him habit train himself in this manner many times (perhaps, shaking his arms and hands furiously, or banging his hands together, etc.). He self-habit trains himself, eventually developing his muscles and coordination. This is always going on at the unconscious and conscious levels from the date of birth and increasingly so every month thereafter.

"When you are teaching baby a system of habits, you must remember that this is the way baby habit trains himself. Before he can acquire a system of habits you want him to master, he must go through a period of self-observation

45

and experience the habit repeatedly before he can accept the habit unconsciously.

"Baby's remarkable ability to self-learn a lot of habit patterns is what makes the human being unique, compared to other forms of life; such as dogs, fishes, insects, etc. This is why human beings can do so many remarkable activities, such as play musical instruments, read books, draw, etc., as these are mainly systems of habits.

"Your baby is constantly, almost daily, developing new habit patterns. These are mostly **physical habits during the first ninety days.**

"After that, you will begin to see social habits emerging and, of course, that is what you and your husband are eagerly expecting. Socially responding is what makes parenting worthwhile. The big day is when baby says, 'ma-ma'.

"At about seven months the baby has sufficient conscious control of bodily movements and social interactions for training. A parent can then definitely begin some training in acts of self-management. Prior to this, baby is weekly creating hundreds of necessary habit patterns for acts of self-management, and survival through self-learning."

Parents Habit Train Baby

I continued to explain to Joan how parents habit train their baby.

"Once baby is sitting up, parents can start teaching him in a very limited way. Habit training will increase weekly and monthly as baby gains more conscious control over his bodily functions. After a certain time, when conscious control has definitely taken over, there will be struggles over whether he will let you boss him. The struggle over being bossed will last for years."

Habit Trainers

"So what you are saying, Dr. Wise, is that during these early months I can relax and just watch my baby forming habit patterns. Exactly what are these habit patterns? What do I look for? I never had a course in child training."

"There is a book that you will want to read by Dr. Arnold Gesell, entitled *The First Five Years of the Preschool Child*. He was one of the early pioneers in child development studies and was the director of the Yale Clinic of Child Development years ago in Connecticut (available: Amazon. com —Print on Demand, only).

"Dr. Gesell studied the maturational patterning of babies and children. He and his staff recorded which patterns emerged, and when. During the first year, these are described as a weekly schedule in his book. This knowledge of maturational patterning will help you and you husband in a variety of ways to adjust as parents.

"From these patterns, you will be able to approximately determine when a habit is about to emerge, so that you can begin to train your child for that habit. Dr. Gesell's book particularly takes the guessing out of consciously training your baby for the first five years. If you know when and what to expect in the stages of maturational patterning, you will know when to train the child in acts of self-management so that both of you will have increasing experiences of success. In addition to Dr. Gesell's studies, the following systems are learned and acquired, developed, and used by every infant to become an adult:

- The autonomic system
- Maturational patterning
- The conscious and unconscious mind
- Authority relationships

47

- Systems of habits
- Self-observation"

I further explained to Joan, "You do not need to know the scientific theories behind each system. I mention these concepts merely for you to understand that they do exist. When a parent learns to use these systems interchangeably, they become an effective habit trainer."

"Doctor, I never thought habit training was that important in the life of a baby, or a child. I certainly never thought of looking for a book like Dr. Gesell's, to anticipate maturational patterning or developing self-management systems in my child. I was just thinking of bottles, diapers, cooking, and loving. When I think of habits, I think of bad habits. I don't know why that should be. I guess because I have never heard any one talk about habit training a baby."

"Joan, many mothers never consider the fact that a child must be constantly and consistently habit trained. The fault lies when we condition ourselves to think some habits of eating, drinking, and smoking are bad. Then, we make the mistake of thinking all habits are bad and not something to acquire.

"For a mother to successfully habit train her child, the child must first be able to control himself and second, he needs to allow his mother to boss him when learning acts of self-management. He also needs to be pressured by the parent to follow a routine, until that routine becomes automatic."

Since habit training was a new idea to Joan, she had few ideas of what to do to train her child in acts of self-management, other than to use a trial and error method. So I further explained, "Joan, a mother, by necessity, is a habit trainer. She must understand habit training in order for her child to be superior in self-management."

"Until now, Doctor, I never had an image of myself as being a habit trainer. I know habits are important. I know I have habits. I never thought too much about habit training myself or how I got my habits, let alone trying to habit train a child."

"Well, Joan, habits are sneaky. They start when you are not looking and get a good hold on you. Then they say, 'ha, ha, you don't even know that I'm around'. This is true because when self-learning as a child, the child has no idea he is acquiring habits. So he grows up unaware of what has happened. When someone says to him, 'Why do you always do that?' The child shrugs his shoulders and says, 'I don't know.'

"Further, parents do not say to a child, 'Today I'm going to teach you a habit or a group of habits.' Nor do teachers tell their students in the classroom, 'Today I will teach these habit patterns.' Parents and teachers do not classify what they are doing because they do not recognize that they are teaching systems of habits or that they are habit trainers. Learning how to teach habits is one of the most important and rewarding aspects of being a parent or teacher."

Since Joan was a newcomer to self-management techniques, I knew she needed me to tell her how a mother goes about habit training her child.

Toilet Training

Toilet training is a complicated act of self-management. It takes so long for a child to learn all the systems of habits that finally make it possible for the toddler to urinate or to defecate in a toilet bowl.

Baby doesn't care if he urinates or defecates in a toilet. If no one trains him to do otherwise, he will continue to urinate in his diapers, as long as mother changes him. Toilet training is all mother's idea.

When cloth was invented, it didn't take mom long to figure out how to make a diaper since she had been urinated on enough. Her shelter (be it a cave, log cabin, tent, or house over the millennium) had smelled up enough by her child's urination and defecation to want a solution. Diapers were just the answer.

Diapers have to be washed and when you are having one baby after another, this is a most unpleasant task. So every mother pushes to toilet train her child.

The first month baby seems to urinate every hour. Thank God for disposable diapers as Mother know that she cannot train baby yet. So she just cooperates with his **autonomic system** by changing baby's diapers.

Maturational Patterns

After three months, Mother observes that her infant is now urinating at two to three hour intervals. She is learning about **maturational patterns** that will give baby more and more control over himself. She is also developing an instinct to catch the clue baby signals when he urinates.

Recognizing Clues

The conscious and unconscious systems also give clues to mother. From experience, she looks for clues that tell her when baby is ready to dirty his diapers. Eventually she differentiates between bowel and urination signals.

Baby also begins to consciously know the signal that his autonomic system gives him for urination. He becomes fussy or irritable (signals may vary from child to child). He fusses when his diapers are wet. Mother, by changing his diapers whenever he is wet, has already begun toilet training him.

Then one day mother notices baby becoming very quiet, red-faced, not wanting to be bothered as his eyes become starry-eyed, looking off into space. From experience she knows what is happening. She rushes him off to the toilet to place baby's first golden nuggets into a bowl. Eventually baby gives mother signals when he is done. In time he gives her signals before he urinates or defecates in his diapers.

This is a significant factor in toilet training. There is a maturational time for this signaling to happen. If mother doesn't know what to look for, she will miss the signals and potty training may take much longer to achieve.

Then one day another milestone arrives. Baby is regularly sitting up in his crib. His conscious and unconscious minds are cooperating. Then comes the time when he is standing up. It is now that some mothers begin toilet training even though he can't walk or say enough words. At this stage baby is totally dependent on mother. He is not aware of when he is going to urinate or defecate. Mother just watches for clues to be successful some of the time. She is the one being habit trained, not baby. Baby is really ready to be toilet trained when he is walking and talking. It takes a lot of communication to learn the necessary systems of toilet training.

Mother learns that she can't complete toilet training until all the maturational patterns have emerged. When her child can walk to the potty chair, he can be toilet trained. He has learned by self-observation when it is time to tell mother. This seems to be accidental learning, but it is not.

Mother plops him on the potty chair. He at first likes this idea. She slips his potty tray in front of him and quickly hands him a toy or thing to amuse him. Soon mother hears, tinkle, tinkle. Baby hears it too, looking wide-eyed and surprised. Mother smiles. So baby smiles. She has him stand and observe what he has done. She praises him because he has no reason to sit on a chair and urinate. He is doing her a favor. He doesn't know it, but he is being **dethroned**. He is giving up his control which was based on his helplessness.

By placing baby on the potty chair when he is ready, mother eventually trains him to request his chair rather than his diapers. He will, in time, anticipate and hold back his urine or BM . Then he will run to mother so that she can take off his diapers and plop him on the potty chair.

Mother provides the routine of consistency to toilet train her child. It is the steady pressure of the parent that produces the habit. If he refuses to follow the routine, he must be enticed to do so until the habit is automatic. There are many factors that come together before a baby is toilet trained. Until he can walk and has words to communicate with, he has to depend on others."

Joan was amazed and had no idea at the complexity of toilet training a child. She was convinced that she, or any other parent, must learn to become a habit trainer.

Chapter 6

Teaching Children Habits

PALE (A System Of Habits)

At the end of Joan's last therapy session, she was unsure of how to recognize a **system of habits** and what it entailed. In order to be a good habit trainer, she needed to know what habits were and how they are acquired.

During the many years as a psychologist in private practice, I learned that in order to help my patients, I needed to develop a system they could relate too. Through trial and error, I discovered that every habit is composed of four systems, which I called PALE.

In order to develop a habit, one, some, or the four systems need to be used.

A System Of Habits

P	**Physical**
A	**Authority Relationship**
L	**Language**
E	**Emotional**

They do not necessarily occur in this order.

At Joan's next appointment, I explained the four systems of habits called PALE.

"Joan, habits are made up of repeatable activities. When all parts of a habit are mastered, it becomes automatic."

"But what are these habits you are talking about, Doctor?"

"Okay, Joan, let's use the PALE system of habits so that you will rapidly catch on to how habits are developed. Can you tell me what happens when a child opens the door for the first time?

"Well, Doctor, I never thought about it before."

"Joan, to explain how PALE works, we will explore what happens when a child learns to open a door. You will then have a better idea of how to apply PALE to many other systems of habits, like riding a bike, flying a kite, etc."

P

P is for physical actions. Opening a door requires using **physical actions.** When a child attempts to open the door, he already has a number of physical abilities to help him. He can push or he can pull; he knows how to turn his wrist; he is already walking; and he knows how to step backwards—all of which he will use when opening the door.

Now all the child has to do is put these pre-learned physical abilities to work for him when he opens the door. He must learn to use a sequence of physical actions. While learning to open a door, the child goes through a lot of frustration which causes him to sometimes cry.

Accidentally is generally how a child learns most of his habits. In learning to open the door, the child uses previously learned **physical patterns** which he puts together to learn the new system.

Curiosity in the child is a great help to all mothers. When baby begins to walk, curiosity helps him discover the door and particularly the knob. At first he just touches it. Then he discovers it can turn. The toddler's curiosity helps him to develop habits, which start with self-discovery and are mostly accidental.

PALE (A System Of Habits)

Pushing the door shut is quickly learned and enjoyed. Little children often chuckle as the door slams. To open the door is more difficult and sometimes causes lots of frustration. After many frustrating tries, baby discovers that the knob turns in either direction. He may think, 'what do I do now, the door is still closed' The real difficulty is learning to turn the knob and to pull the door at the same time. If the child forgets to step backwards, the door will open too fast. This will cause the door to bump up against him, pushing him over, thus closing again. The toddler feels very frustrated and cries many times as he falls down repeatedly trying to open the door.

Eventually the child remembers in which direction to pull the door and in which direction to turn the knob while taking a step backwards. He finally learns to open the door through many trials and errors. After awhile the patterns of physical actions become automatic.

Until the total **system of physical actions** becomes automatic, both mother and child suffer repeated frustration. It takes many weeks to learn the system of physical habits before the child masters opening the door.

When you see your child opening the door with ease, then your know the physical habits for opening a door has been mastered.

A

A is for the five authority relationships.
> **Bossing Another**
> **Being Bossed**
> **Bossing Myself**
> **Delegated Authority**
> **Impersonal Authority**

They are always used in learning any system of actions or system of habits. These authority relationships are constantly occurring all during the day for every human being and in almost every activity. The five authority relationships apply to opening a door?"

"Joan, if you ask your child to open the door for the very first time, do you think he will do it?

"Oh, I guess he would. I don't see why he wouldn't."

"Just stop for a moment and think. I think he is liable to say, 'no,' or he may ignore you."

"Now why would he do that?"

"He doesn't know how to open the door. Besides, why should he be obedient to do something he knows nothing about?"

"You're right, Doctor."

L

L is for using a language system. Opening a door requires another system of PALE. The toddler has already been using words and applying these sound patterns to objects long before learning to open a door.

The child learns to say 'door.' Then the toddler learns to distinguish between the 'back' door and the 'front' door and to say these two words and phrases. There are words like 'open' and 'close' as well as 'knob,' to apply to this situation.

There are verbal courtesies that accompany the five authority relationships; such as — please open the door, thank you for closing the door, excuse me for interrupting, but could you open the door. These are the magical words of consideration.

E

E is for the system of emotions. Emotions accompany the learning of physical actions. Mother helps her child learn emotional control from the day he is born. One wonders why a child keeps trying to overcome the frustrations necessary to learn a **system of physical actions**, such as to ride a trike, to pull a toy duck on a string, to walk up stairs, to hold a spoon and put food in the mouth. The list goes on and on as there are countless physical actions to be acquired by a child, which almost alway causes mother and baby emotional frustration.

The four systems of PALE (physical systems, authority relationships, language, and emotional systems) are all intertwined like an invisible web. When a parent uses authority relationships, the other three systems of PALE are also used simultaneously.

"Dr. Wise, if much of this learning is self-discovery and accidental learning, what do I do to help my child?"

"Well, Joan, you are there to aid your child emotionally as he masters each frustrating pattern necessary to open the door. You are there to encourage and perhaps to explain a part of the system he is not getting: like stepping backwards at the same time he turns the knob and pulls the door towards him. You can pick up your child, soothe and help him to try again. You can also take his hand and help him turn the knob as a way of alleviating frustration. It takes years to learn a system of emotional control thoroughly. You can help your child gain the emotional stability he needs when going through frustrating experiences of learning a system of habits. Some children will need little coaching, others will need a lot more. It will depend on how well a child's previous habits have been learned. And, of course, how much self-confidence he has in himself at this age. Gradually, Joan, you will teach your child to use PALE to open the door. Slowly, you will create habits of obedience (child being bossed) or you will be frustrated by your child's response to your request."

"How do I create habits of obedience, Doctor?"

Habits Of Obedience
"A child must be trained to be willing to carry out an action when requested to do so by a parent. This is called habits of obedience which must be well learned. Every parent is aware of this difficult task of getting a child to willingly comply with a request. This is a cooperative action that must become a habitual response. A child is more likely to respond to a stranger or a friend when asked to open or close a door, rather than a parent."

"Why is that, Dr. Wise?"

"I guess the child feels as though a parent is his sole possession. Being the 'little king' also places him in a position of accepting or refusing his subject's request. If he feels like it, he will, and if he doesn't, he won't. A lot of this accepting and rejecting has to do with whether or not the child has had similar PALE experiences and whether or not he is in an obedient mood. Many times a mother must demand that the child complies with her request. If she handles an obedience situation correctly, the child creates habits of obedience."

PALE (A System Of Habits)

"Is this like dethroning the child?"

"Yes, it is part of the dethroning process, Joan. This is when the child finds out that he must put away his 'little king' role and become responsible for his actions."

"Dr. Wise, I definitely was not prepared for the ideas of habit training my child. When I train my child to accept a system of habits, I now know that I will be teaching these four systems of PALE — Physical, Authority Relationships, Language, and Emotional. It all seems too much."

"I know, Joan. When you are a beginning mother, there often seems to be too much to be learned. Fortunately, baby is not in a hurry much of the time, so you have lots of time to adjust and learn."

"I can see that understanding PALE will help mothers teach their children to learn the four systems of habits for such activities as riding a trike, catching a ball, and the many other skills that a child must learn. I never thought of or heard about your systems of habits, nor have I ever heard of mothers being habit trainers. But, I can see it is true. It is just common sense for mothers to be habit trainers."

"Joan, prior to age two and a half, the toddler is learning parts of PALE. Usually in an accidental sort of way, and parts of these systems are self-learned. Like using alphabet blocks. At first, baby is lucky to get one block stacked on top of another block."

"Doctor, when does the child learn a system of habits in a short period of time?

"I guess it just depends upon how simple the skill is and the age of the child. At any age there are some systems that are learned almost instantly. After age three and a half, the systems can be learned faster as the parent can very definitely now teach a part or parts of a system to the child. The child also increasingly learns from other children. The child now no longer depends upon self-learning exclusively.

"A five and a half year old is mastering parts of the four systems of PALE to an adequate degree. Each week he increases the number of systems he knows. He is now being taught by teachers at kindergarten. Many boys and girls can read, swim, ride bikes, play games on the Internet, etc."

Joan looked surprised at this point, and commented, "All of this requires a lot more patience, foresight, and analysis than I thought necessary to become a mother. I thought much of this just happened naturally; that baby somehow learned things by himself. Being a mother requires a lot of skill, know-how, and particularly, analytical ability. Thank goodness the Creator has granted mothers and children time enough to figure out really complicated systems of patterns."

"Joan, this is just the beginning in teaching habits. I would like to introduce a very important concept. The concept of **consistency** which will help you to be a successful habit trainer. In order to be consistent you need to understand that the conscious and subconscious minds play a large part in controlling the systems of self-management."

Consistency (Conscious & Subconscious Minds)

In today's world of technology, a missing part in a software program is called a bug or glitch. Sometimes it takes programmers weeks or months to find the missing link or

PALE (A System Of Habits)

links to correct it. This causes frustration to the programmer, his boss, and the end user as everything stops until the bug or bugs are eliminated. When only a part of the system of habits is learned by the child, the same thing happens, everything stops, frustration sets in until the missing part or parts are learned.

Habits or habit patterns connect the conscious and the subconscious minds. Every child is shifting in a variety of ways between the conscious and the subconscious minds. How consistent a system of habits is practiced by the child determines the success of the system. It also determines whether or not the subconscious mind accepts the system.

Consistency in practicing habits determines whether a particular relationship between parent and child is harmonious or disturbing. This is why a child should naturally keep repeating the chosen system over and over until the consistency reaches a level of reliability to avoid disharmony or failure.

However, the conscious mind of the parent or child may settle for learning only a part of a system of habits. Either the subconscious mind or the experience of the external system of habits will send a message of frustration (pain) to the brain telling the child that the system is not thoroughly learned; that only part of the system is learned. The subconscious mind (the living computer) will not let the child take the next step in the system unless the previous step is reliably performed. This is nature's way of preventing a more serious problem. The child can ignore this signal of frustration or he can do something about it. Many times a child will give a warning to the parent by crying.

Many times when a child is not successful at school or at home, the fault lies in the fact that not enough systems

61

of habits are taught. Thereby, the child becomes frustrated (pained), not knowing that several more thoroughly learned steps are necessary. The teacher teaches the child many systems of habits each day. The parent and child fail to realize, for whatever reason, that each part of a system must be practiced until a certain level of consistency is reached to automatically make the system work. Many times the teacher will fail to pressure a child to learn a particular part of a system to a necessary level of consistency because of limited time or lack of interest on the part of the child.

Further, I explained to Joan why consistency in teaching habits is so important and how the conscious and subconscious mind play their part in catching habits that are faulty.

"I get it now, Dr. Wise. There are systems of habits for all kinds of acts of self-management: like brushing teeth, washing hands, going to bed, putting objects back where they belong, etc. A parent must teach the child many organized systems. I also understand that the systems must fit together using all the parts and each part mastered by the child or he will become anxious until he masters the missing parts."

Breaking The Whole Into Parts
"That's right, Joan. When a parent habit trains a child to do an activity such as a jigsaw puzzle, the parent begins by breaking the total system up into four parts according to the four systems of PALE which I have just explained:

P   Recognizing the physical relationships of the pieces;
A   Practicing the five systems of authority relationships;
L   Learning the language of puzzle solving;
E   Emotionally controlling oneself when a piece won't fit."

PALE (A System Of Habits)

See how the five authority relationships work when putting a puzzle together. First, a person needs to boss himself to find the pieces and boss himself to put the puzzle away after he is done with it. If he is putting the puzzle together with another person, that person may boss him as to what section he will work on, or vice versa.

What a parent is teaching a child by doing puzzles is that a whole can be divided into parts. In this case a picture is divided into parts. One can take the parts, fit these together, and get the whole. It is a necessary intellectual relationship that a child must perceive, seeing the physical relationships of the parts of a picture.

The first step in fitting the pieces together is to have a child look at the picture to see how the pieces fit together. The child must know what parts to look for in the picture before beginning to fit the pieces. This is usually the first failure in puzzle solving if you do not follow this procedure.

A parent teaches the child to look at the objects in the picture, noting the colors, size, and location of the objects. This is a habit that a parent helps the child to practice and is a step in the system of physical relationships for puzzles that a child is forced to learn.

The objective of the puzzle maker is to make a number of pieces to confuse the assembler. Printed on the box is the number of pieces of the puzzle which tells the assembler how difficult the puzzle will be. Parents pick a puzzle according to the number of pieces and the age of the child. Under four years of age, the parents pick a puzzle with three to ten pieces. For an older child, the parent picks a puzzle with fifty, one hundred or five hundred pieces depending upon the child's age.

A child of seven can solve a puzzle of fifty pieces by observing more accurately the system of physical relationships. He looks for the pieces that form the sides of the picture and the corners. This will aid him in putting the puzzle together. The child looks for matching pieces of the same color. The child determines from looking at the picture on the box whether it is a square, a circle, or a rectangle. The child looks for several pieces that form a big object in the picture. If a parent teaches the child to look for all of these details, the child will apply the PALE system successfully."

"Dr, Wise, you have convinced me. Thank goodness I have years to prepare myself to be a habit trainer. I also have time to create better habits for myself," Joan said as she sat back in her chair with a look of contentment on her face.

I knew from Joan's actions that I had done my job. I had reduced her anxieties and fears about training her child. I had also shown her that parents are habit trainers. Habit trainers create a way of life for the child that is interesting, full of fun, and full of hope. The habit trainer reduces not only future adult fears and anxieties of a child, but the child's current fears and anxieties as well, by knowing how to teach the system of habits for acts of self-management. Parents and child both benefit when the parent becomes an excellent habit trainer.

Chapter 7

Training Baby Out Of Helplessness

Overcoming Helplessness

Overcoming helplessness is not just a matter of teaching a child a new system of habits or a new act of self-management, but learning how to overcome the feelings of fear, real or imagined. Fear produces a natural feeling of helplessness when one doesn't know how to do something. It doesn't mean that a child or adult should feel inferior or dumb because he or she has not yet mastered a new habit or act.

It is important to teach the child a method to overcome helpless feelings, as they are a constant and a never-ending problem for every person from birth until the end of life. Many times a person is overwhelmed by these feelings whenever faced with new situations or sometimes for no apparent reason. Until the child or the adult can master a method of overcoming this crippling emotion of helplessness, he or she can never be fully independent.

Feelings Of Helplessness

Every pre-schooler has deep seated feelings of helplessness for a variety of reasons. These feelings are well grounded after the first three years of living, as baby is born helpless. He is born inferior to other human beings. He can't walk. He can't talk. He gets teased. He is called names. He doesn't learn fast enough. He compares himself to other children older than himself. Kids tell him, "You are too small. You are too fat." All these comments make him feel inferior and helpless. This is so because the ability to reason things out has not yet developed. Every pre-schooler has a history of being truly dependent.

There are many ways in which a parent teaches a baby or child to overcome helplessness. During the pre-verbal span of time, before rational understanding occurs, a parent helps the child overcome helplessness by smiling, hugging, clapping hands, and assisting the baby to be successful and to feel secure in his environment. **After five and a half**, when the child has enough words and experiences to understand explanations, the process of overcoming helplessness can be explained.

Diminishing Helplessness

Fortunately, there are steadily growing experiences of independence in the child from birth on.

Sometimes children play that they are superman or superwoman. These delusions of grandeur and power are an aid to defeat the feelings of helplessness that every pre-schooler feels. This helps them want to be independent, not dependent.

Many pre-schoolers want to do whatever they see an adult do, like play an instrument, drive a car, catch and hit a ball. To them it looks easy. They naturally try to do what the adult is doing, but unfortunately fail.

This scenario happens many times to a child or teenager. He doesn't understand how much training it takes to do something that appears effortless. If he knew how much effort and training was required to perform an activity, he would know that he was not a failure.

This is a serious misconception on the child's part. With enough failures, the child begins to think that learning a new activity is too difficult. It is then easy to say, "I can't do it."

Training Baby Out of Helplessness

Sometimes the parent without realizing it, emphasizes the child's helplessness or the child's ability to overcome helpless feelings. Instead the parent needs to encourage the child to believe, **"It may not be as easy as it looks, but if you learn it a step at a time, you can do it. If you keep trying, you will get it."**

These are the kind of statements a parent must tell the child, and, if necessary, have the child repeat a new learning activity. As the child succeeds in using the step by step method, he becomes successful in how to handle learning new activities. This is how a parent builds self-confidence and helps the child overcome feelings of helplessness.

Once a child understands and accepts the idea of breaking a new activity down into learning steps, his feelings of helplessness will diminish. The parent can then explain all of the steps that are necessary to learn that activity. This gives the child a plan of operation. In this way, there are no unexpected surprises as most activities are made up of parts. In time, the child learns to break the activity down into parts for himself.

Breaking An Activity Into Parts

Let's take roller skating as a way of understanding the process of overcoming the natural feelings of helplessness. The child, because he feels helpless on skates for the first time, may not want to try.

First, one must learn to stand on skates. Then a certain amount of balance and experience is needed to take a step before taking the next step. How much experience is required for each step depends upon the child. What the child is doing during each step is passing from erratic movements to smooth movements.

What causes the erratic movements? Uncertainty, not knowing whether to take a big step or a small step or where to put the foot after a step has been taken. Fear of making a mistake, fear of self-disapproval as well as expecting external disapproval, lack of experience, and expecting to get it right with the first try — all of these create awkward, erratic movements.

Therefore, the parent teaches the child to expect erratic movement when learning an act or system for the first time. This is a way of building self-confidence. Once the child understands the procedure, he will approach a new learning situation with confidence, not a feeling of helplessness.

After enough repetition of steps and sliding along, the child passes from consciously trying to learn the action to unconscious smooth movements. Enough experience with each step will vanish the fear and uncertainty.

The parent stands in front of the child holding his two hands so that he gets the feeling of standing on rolling wheels, the feeling of boots attached to wheels, and the feeling of heavy weights on his legs and feet.

Now the parent pulls the child by the two hands a short distance with both feet together — just to let him get the feeling of rolling and balancing on skates.

For some children, this may be enough to learn for one day. Five minutes is probably enough. An older child may be able to do more the first time. After awhile, the child as well as the parent learns how much time to practice a step before advancing to the next step. At first, the child depends upon mother's or father's judgment.

The next practice session repeats the steps of the first session and then adds to it. The parent has the child walk on skates across the carpet. This is a good way to gain balance.

Training Baby Out of Helplessness

Falling on the carpet, as he will find out, does not hurt very much.

Another way is to tie a rope from one end of the porch to the other and have the child hold on to it while pulling himself across. The child must learn to balance himself before he can feel secure in skating by himself. If he falls while pulling himself across the porch, he can hold on to the rope while sliding down to the ground. His fear of falling is diminishing while he learns to balance himself.

The final step in learning to skate is when the child lets go of all supports to skate on his very own. "Can I do it on my own?" he keeps asking himself. When he can answer, "Yes. I know I can," all fear vanishes from his mind at that moment. He skates to his parent, or to a wall, or a chair. Success. He made it. He can take rolling steps now. As the parent keeps encouraging the child to take more rolling steps, self-confidence grows with each successful step.

The child should be aware that he can learn almost any activity if he breaks the system into its parts. Each part must be practiced and mastered before proceeding to the next step.

The Importance Of Repetition & Practice

The parent is always there reassuring the child. Reminding him that one must experience each step enough times to feel self-confidence. The parent explains to the child that he must keep repeating a small step at a time until it is mastered. Two words a child eventually learns are "repetition" and "practice." These words and the use of them are the keys necessary to get a child or anyone out of the state of helplessness. At first the child cannot understand the importance of these two words. But by the time he masters at least one system of habits, he will get the idea of how important they are.

Children are usually in a hurry to learn. They don't want to take each step and repeat the skill of that step again and again until it is mastered. Each step must be mastered to gain the necessary experience and skill before proceeding to the next step.

When enough systems of habits are acquired, the child may not feel helpless when learning a new activity or going through a change in situations. From experience, he knows he is in a state of ignorance because the situation is new to him. This is an important insight and a big step forward as the child **feels confident** that if another person helps or teaches him, or if he can figure it out by himself, given the time, he will be able to learn the new activity — such as riding a bike, swimming, doing some kind of mathematical problem, etc.

There is an important distinction to be observed regarding helplessness. There's the **feeling of helplessness** and the **state of helplessness**. One is a state of fear while the other is a state of ignorance.

Inferiority Feelings Interfere With Learning

Some parents tend to skip steps or rush the child through a step. The child properly protests many times, only to have his protests ignored. Sometimes the child is ridiculed for protesting. He is pressured to do the next step in spite of protesting.

Some parents, by nature, are impatient and expect too much from the child, increasing the child's feelings of helplessness. They get disturbed when the child makes a mistake. They holler. Get angry. This, too, makes the child feel helpless, and he may not want the parent to teach him anything.

Sometimes a parent thinks that a child can learn complicated skills immediately. If the child doesn't do it speedily, then the parent thinks, and many times will say, "You're dumb," or "You're awkward," or "You're backward." The child feels belittled. Such comments makes the child feel more helpless than he already feels. Now the child will say, "I can't do it," to avoid a feared belittling experience. Remember the child has years of experience in feeling inferior. These remarks will only continue these feelings.

Inferiority feelings interfere with any child learning to boss himself. Although a person may manage an activity properly, he may not enjoy the activity if feelings of inferiority continue, even though the person is now competent.

There is no hurry to get the child to learn. If he never learns to skate, so what. If it takes two months, so what — he is not going to earn money skating. It is just a fun activity. So let the child learn in his own time.

Determination

Sometimes a child with little experience in being successful will be enthusiastic when learning to ride a bike until he falls off because he could not balance himself. He gives up with feelings of helplessness and no desire to try again. This child will remain in the state of helplessness unless he gets rid of his feelings of helplessness by getting back on the bike to try again. This child has no idea why he failed.

Another child after falling down will get right back up on the bike and have no fear of falling or no fear of feeling helpless. He knows he can do it, once he learns how to balance himself. This child has what is called determination and foresight.

To overcome feelings of helplessness and the state of helplessness, one needs determination. How does a parent enhance determination in a child? It exists in every baby and child, but some children have more determination than other children. Parents either encourage or discourage determination without even knowing it.

The parent who expects fast, easy learning probably will not develop determination in the child, but just the opposite.

The parent who explains the meaning of words and how to do a certain activity, step by step, is encouraging and developing determination in the child. After repeated explanations in various learning situations, the child begins to experience success and knows that if he tries, he can do it.

By following this procedure, the parent reduces the fear of failure, which in turn helps the child overcome a lot of helpless feelings of inadequacy and reduces the helpless state.

The adult also assures the child that it doesn't matter if he doesn't get it the first time. The important thing is that the child try until he gets it.

After a child has been encouraged enough times to overcome a helpless feeling by just trying without too much expectation of success, he is learning to build a repertoire of experiences from which to build his determination to keep trying. By doing this, he learns how important it is to overcome helpless feelings and the helpless state.

A fearful child has usually little determination. His helpless feelings are too great. To help him overcome his fear while developing determination requires familiarization with whatever caused him to feel helpless in the first place.

Training Baby Out of Helplessness

If a child is afraid of a swimming pool, he begins to familiarize himself with water by wading into a pool to get used to playing around in water and having lots of fun. For several days he may be content to just wade around, sit in the water and play with toys. The child naturally will see other children playing in the shallow water and having lots of fun. He begins to associate pleasure with water instead of fear.

Eventually the child's fear of water will start to diminish and he will enter the shallow end of the pool by himself. When he looks like he is having a great time splashing and kicking, he can be encouraged to put his head in the water to blow bubbles. In time, the child will learn to swim as his determination increases and his fear of water diminishes.

Many teenagers are successful until they graduate from high school as they have been depending upon the determination or control of the parent. Then they fail in college, or at a job or marriage, as their self-determination has not been steadily growing from birth until graduation. Another factor is that after graduation from high school, many teenagers move out of the family home with glee expecting to take better care of themselves but only to find that they can't cope. During high school days the teenagers had only to earn grades. Their parents made it too easy for them. The child did not experience enough serious difficulties to develop superior determination or training in developing determination.

Some parents don't know how to help the child overcome feelings of helplessness so they protect the child from these feelings and restrict him so that he doesn't have to experience anything new. This stifles the child from developing determination.

Independence comes also through being able to properly handle all five authority relationships. While independence is achieved through learning to boss oneself and to self-manage, no person is completely independent.

The child who refuses to be bossed will not learn the norms of independence for his age level. He will probably be uncooperative at times in the classroom and on the school grounds. He may not be able to regulate himself by rules and routines and will not be very independent. Down the road, some supervisor will always have to observe him, to be sure he follows regulations, policies, rules, or laws.

If a child's parent is one of four types — overprotective, dependent, domineering, or alcoholic, he will find it difficult to achieve independence through self-management.

Sometimes this child can only achieve independence by escaping from a parent; by staying away from home as much as possible, by getting involved in activities outside the home, by being very secretive, by not talking, or by lying. Sometimes the child tries to get independence by quarreling, fighting, or running away. Sometimes other adults through various ruses help a child to achieve some degree of independence. The real escape for a child caught in relationships with any of these four types of parents is through psychotherapy for the parent and the child.

Real independence is worth the price. This is probably why many children and adults fight for it.

Chapter 8

Independence Through
Self-Control

Acquiring Independence

"Carol, how many times have I told you not to leave your bike in the driveway!" father yelled, unable to drive his car into the driveway. Father's thoughts at the moment were that Carol was being thoughtless and disobedient. He was puzzled by her forgetfulness as he had reminded her many times not to leave her bike in the driveway.

Every parent wants their child to become independent as did Carol's father. Parents may not realize that as long as they keep reminding the child, the parent is still bossing, still being responsible, thereby continuing the child's dependency.

It never occurred to the father that his daughter was failing to achieve independence. You see, frequent reminders from parents serve to keep children dependent on them. Carol was forcing her father to boss her repeatedly and was forcing him to be responsible for her behavior. Independence for a child comes through controlling oneself, not being dependent on the authority of a parent or teacher. When a child is able to exercise an act of self-management, he or she is responsible for that act.

Few parents have thought out what is meant by independence, specifically in terms of acts of self-management for each year, such as being able to dress oneself by age six or being able to walk between one and two years of age.

There are so many systems of habits to be acquired by the baby, child, and teenager during the growing years to reach what seems, at times, a vague status of independence.

Each year a child acquires more and more independence.

In the back of the book is a copy of "This Is A Mature Adult." It was written as an answer, years ago, to a group of parents who wanted to know what independence meant. Posting this statement on your child's wall will give him some idea about what he is trying to achieve.

How Independence Is Achieved

Independence is achieved habit by habit, act by act, year after year by the parent bossing the child until the child can boss himself. Independence is accomplished through the gradual shifting of responsibilities from parent to child.

From the moment of conception, baby manages himself and increases his self-management yearly by self-learning a variety of activities and habits. Some activities and habits are learned as he matures from experience with parents, teachers, and other persons.

Humans acquire habits for two reasons: out of necessity or for pleasure. The question for parent and child is not whether or not he wants to boss himself, but whether a particular system of habits or activities is worth acquiring.

Many times a child will refuse to acquire a system of habits that the parent deems necessary. This can be very frustrating to the parent who may feel pressured, at times, to force the child to acquire the habit.

Sometimes the refusal by the child will be caused by faulty parenting techniques, by a lack of knowledge on the part of a parent or child, by reasons of biochemistry, or peer pressure.

Viewed as an adult, such acts of self-management like music, dance, sports, art, etc. are all desirable and beneficial. However, viewed as a child, such acts may not be worth acquiring. Sometimes either a parent, a teacher, or another adult will convince the child that one of the arts is worth-while. But, after a few lessons, when the child sees how many hours he will need to practice to acquire this system of habits, he quite sensibly wants to quit. This then becomes a challenge to the parent. The parent can become very dis-appointed and frustrated by the child's wanting to quit but, on the other hand, so can the child become frustrated and unhappy because of the parent's persistence. Since the child sees no benefit at that time he logically wants to quit.

Sometimes a parent can successfully pressure a child into an activity he refuses to learn and many years later he will thank the parent for forcing him. Unfortunately, there are too many activities and habits for the child to learn for a parent to do this too often. If negative relationships exists between parent and child, the parent will obviously lose more often than not.

If cooperative relationships are created in the pre-school years, the parent will more often win in these discretionary activities, such as sports, the arts, or a variety of other activities. One of the keys then to independence is cooperative relationships.

The other key is shifting the responsibility for the child's actions, decisions, and welfare from the parent to the child.

Failing To Shift Responsibilities

Usually the parent is definitely trying to shift the respon-sibility, but for one reason or another many parents do not succeed. Why? How do parents prevent the gradual shifting of responsibilities from parent to child?

Well, let's start from the beginning. At first it is fun for mother to be totally responsible for such a helpless little doll. It makes her feel very important and fulfills a need inside of her. Some mothers enjoy this activity so much that they refuse to let the baby become independent — but not so for other mothers.

As time passes this helpless infant grows taller and heavier. There are many diapers to change and the cleaning up of baby becomes a chore. At first, breast or bottle feeding is a great joy, but when mother is awakened two and three times a night to feed a hungry infant, this gets to be tiresome. The house begins to show lack of attention because infant needs to be held so much of the time. Mother begins to look tired from lack of sleep and many times is exhausted. There are always so many demands. The baby is always crying, the baby is hungry, the baby is dirty, the baby is into something. This parent is having difficulty knowing when to shift responsibility to her child. In desperation she pops the bottle of milk on a pillow and lets him feed himself so that she can do something else.

Fear & Guilt

Then as mother encourages baby to take care of himself in some small way, there is some friend who will question what she is doing and makes her feel guilty for not prolonging baby's dependency. It goes something like this: A friend sees the baby lying in his crib feeding himself and remarks, "Oh, are you not supposed to hold the baby so that he feels secure while eating?" Mother immediately feels guilty even though she only does this occasionally.

Mother gives the baby a spoon to feed himself, thinking that's a great idea. Again, a person says, "Isn't he too young to eat by himself. He is liable to swallow it."

Mother may leave the baby with a babysitter only to have her baby scream as she walks out the door. Mother again feels guilty. She thinks, "Is he too young to leave with the babysitter?"

Independence Through Self-Control

Fathers frequently will not let their child ride a bike out of fear of accidents.

Other parents, due to fear of drowning, will not let their child learn to swim and engage in water sports.

Fears of what might happen to a child causes the overprotective parent to prevent the shifting of responsibility of self-care to the child. People say ridiculous things, and the mother feels guilty for letting her child be independent in small ways. So the parent many times, for a variety of reasons, is reluctant to shift the responsibility.

The Needy Parent

Needing emotional response and liking to take care of a child blinds some mothers to letting the child care for himself when he is ready. Some mothers especially like the pre-school phase of childhood as they really don't want the child to grow up.

Some mothers would like to keep their child at a certain age. This desire to keep the child from maturing does stunt the child's human relationship growth and emotional development. Fortunately, the physical growth of the child continues to develop. Some women have no other purpose in life than to be a parent, so refuse to give up parenting responsibilities. Some mothers lack affection from their husbands, so hang on to parenting. Some mothers can only get the attention from their husbands through rearing children.

A few first-time mothers spend hours rocking their babies every day causing them to be very dependent. The baby then will cry if he is not held, soothed, and given attention. The baby will find it hard to entertain himself and expect only mother to entertain him. These babies then have to be broken of this dependency.

The reasons for not transferring responsibility to the child are numerous. Sometimes it requires a psychologist to ferret out the reason or reasons to help the mother or the father, or both, let go, so that the normal transition of responsibility can take place.

How To Shift Authority

I had such a family situation in my office a number of years ago, when both parents failed to let the normal transition of responsibility happen.

Mr. and Mrs. Olsen came to my office complaining of the difficulties they were having with their fourteen-year-old son in the morning. They stated they were willing to pay any amount if I would just make their morning hours bearable.

Mr. Olsen explained, "Doctor, my wife and I love our fourteen-year-old son, but we must be doing something wrong as all three of us are so unhappy in the morning hours."

"Tell me, Mr. Olsen. What happens in the morning? Begin with your son getting out of bed and finally leaving for school."

Mr. Olsen groans, "Every morning I go into his room several times to awaken him. The first time I speak nicely, which usually doesn't work. Then I get cross with him. Finally, I have to shake him and pull him out of bed. By this time we are both nasty with each other."

Mother interrupts, "And then my son comes directly to breakfast in his bed clothes, hair not combed, teeth not brushed, face and hands not washed. For years I have been scolding him, but it does no good."

Independence Through Self-Control

Father continues, "Then he starts eating. He is demanding, nasty, and rude. He makes us so unhappy with the way he eats breakfast."

Mrs. Olsen replies, "He then watches TV. I know that he is gong to be late for school. I know that my husband will get upset as he drives him to school because it is too far for him to walk. I get so anxious reminding him to get dressed because he will be late for school. He just ignores me."

Mr. Olsen agrees, "I usually get very angry with him when I see that I am going to be late to work because of him. Then he moves. Finally he gets dressed. Can't find his homework or books. So we all anxiously look for whatever he can't find."

Mrs. Olson adds, "They go out the door quarreling. I do not like to see my husband and son so disturbed with each other."

"I assume, Mr. Olson, you and your son drive to school either silently or in anger."

"That is true, Dr. Wise. I know that my boss will be displeased again as I am late so often. What can we do? Is there anything that can be done? Is it too late?"

"First, let me assure you both that this morning hour is correctable. But be aware that it will require many more changes by both of you, than changes by your son."

"We don't care. We will gladly change," was their reply.

"All right. Then you must give up being responsible for your son's actions. Let him be responsible for his own actions and habits.

Mr. Olsen interrupted, "But that is what we have been trying to do."

81

"I know you have been trying, but let me tell you some ways in which you can shift the responsibility to him for his morning activities. First, get an alarm clock and put it in his room. Let him set the alarm - not you."

"That will not work," said Mr. Olsen. "If I can't get him up, how will that work?"

"At first it may not work, but eventually it will."

"How? They both exclaimed.

I said, "When he gets up late, you don't feed him."

Mother shocked, "And let my boy go to school hungry?"

"Yes," I said. "He must pay a price for not being responsible. This is how he or anyone learns. You learn by paying a price and in this case your boy goes hungry for one meal. Then let him walk to school. He and you are both paying a heavy emotional price now. Missing a meal can actually be healthy for him."

"He will be late to school. I don't want him being late," cried Mr. Olsen.

"That's another price he will have to pay. You have the habit of punctuality, not your son. He still has to acquire it. You can't give it to him. He has to acquire this habit on his own. The school personnel will make him feel uncomfortable about being late, as will his teachers and classmates. Your kindness is preventing him from being self-managed. He is not learning to boss himself. You are still bossing him and he is fighting you every inch of the way.

"The clock is what I call **impersonal authority**. It forces him to boss himself. The clock shifts responsibility from father to son. He must rely on rules and routines to control himself and to achieve independence. This is a shift from personal authority to impersonal authority. None of you will have a peaceful relationship in the morning hours until your son and you do this. In the morning, don't serve him breakfast until he is dressed with hair combed, with face and hands washed."

"He will not do it," both parents replied.

"Then he doesn't eat or watch TV That is the price he pays for not bossing himself. You tell him that this is the routine that is to be followed in the morning from now on. This routine is there so that you don't have to boss him. Tell him that independence comes through bossing himself. Tell him that when he can't follow the routine of the house, he doesn't eat, nor does he watch TV until he does. Tell him that he has a choice - follow the routine of the morning hour or pay the consequence.

"You have been teaching him disobedience by constantly reminding him and not making him pay the price for being disobedient. I prefer you use the words 'bossing yourself' to the word 'disobedient' when you talk to your son. By saying 'disobedient,' you are still maintaining parental authority. He will not learn independence this way. You are preserving his dependency on you by bossing him.

"When you say to your son, 'Can you boss yourself?' you are placing the responsibility on him. He will say, 'yes.' Then tell him, 'Son, tell yourself to get dressed before coming to the breakfast table with hair combed, with teeth brushed, and with hands and face washed.'

"This is a type of impersonal authority you and your wife can use. Impersonal authority helps a child or an adult to be independent. Personal authority, on the other hand, causes a person to be dependent. Personal authority cannot be eliminated, but can certainly be reduced."

"We can't tell him not to watch TV," both parents admitted. "We have already tried that." He will not obey us. He just goes and turns it on."

"If he is that disobedient, you can loan the TV out for awhile until he breaks the bad habit of watching it in the mornings. Parents who are too kind and permit disobedience are problem sufferers and not problem solvers, as you two have become. Both of you are now paying a price. Don't pay the price any longer. Let your son suffer and pay the price so that he can appreciate a solution to his difficulty. You are paying the price along with him. After all these years you have not taught him to boss himself or to be independent. You were so hoping that kindness and reasoning would cause your son to be responsible for his behavior. Sometimes it does work, but not often enough to be relied on as heavily as you have.

"When a child has a cooperative attitude, you can rely on kindness and reason. Your son is neither cooperative or obedient. You have taught him to take advantage of you as you have also taught him to be disobedient. He doesn't have respect for you as parents. You have not taught him that you are worth doing something for."

"How long will this take, Doctor?" Mr. Olsen wanted to know.

"As long as it takes for you to consistently follow through and teach him that you mean what you say. You have taught him to ignore you. It will take time for him to believe that you mean what you are saying. You have some parenting habits to break. You have to learn new ways of controlling your son until he can learn to control himself."

"Well, Mother, do you think that you can do it?" asked Mr. Olsen.

"I can certainly try. The question is, can you do it, my husband?" she asked.

"Well, our way certainly has not worked. What the Doctor says makes good sense to me. Let's give it a try."

It was not easy for Mr. and Mrs. Olsen to shift the responsibility of a fourteen year old from them to their son. Both parents realized that it would take a lot of changing to make it work.

I knew though that they were desperate enough to make the necessary changes. I impressed upon them that if they wait until their son is older, their job would become even more difficult.

In a few weeks the son was honking the horn because father was late. He became independent through bossing himself.

Norms Of Independence

There are norms of independence for every year until eighteen years of age. This is evident in the case of the Olsens. There is no complete list of norms for each year. Dr. Gesell listed a certain number of norms for each year until age ten. When a child attains these norms for his age, he is said to be independent for that age.

There are norms for a span of time and if the person meets these standards for his age group, he is considered mature. When a person reaches eighteen he is considered independent. If a teenager does not meet the standards for his age level, he is called immature.

Being a hermit is considered by some persons as being independent, but this person is not independent as he must withdraw from the community of human beings to escape from his inability to relate to people.

No one is ever really independent. The so-called independent person recognizes that he or she is really dependent on a network of human beings for survival and pleasure.

When a person accepts interdependency and lives up to the norms of independence for his age, we call him mature.

Everyone is interdependent in this environment. Everyone depends upon other human beings, plants, animals, institutions, the air, the water, the soil, etc. to exist. It is as important for a child to recognize that he is interdependent in his environment as he is independent for a particular year or age span. Once a child learns this truth, he will be supportive of a cooperative system of human relationships within or without the family.

Ben Franklin was full of statements that are great for parents and children seeking independence such as, "A stitch in time, saves nine. A bird in the hand is worth two in the bush." Other literary men have also made statements that parents can use to help their children achieve independence.

Chapter 9

Quarreling
(Misuse Of Personal Authority)

Clashes Over Property Rights

"Give me back my truck! It's mine," Bill squawked.

"Let me play with it for a little while," said his older brother.

"No! Give it back to me now!"

"You are a little twerp and a big baby," big brother retaliates.

Bill hits his older brother and screams, "Mom! Don won't give my truck back! Make him give it back!"

This is a familiar scenario every mother hears with two or more children. The clash of personal authority over property rights makes a mother wonder whether to intervene or not. This is a constant dilemma that both mothers and fathers face. Parents cannot escape being involved in these frequent clashes over property and personal rights. Children are great at playing oneupmanship with each other. They are always vying to see who is better and who can beat the other.

The constant personal authority battle that the child is always encountering with mother, more than with dad, is enough to give mother a headache or to have her wish for a holiday by herself. Thank God there are days when children are quiet, cooperative, and a joy. This is a welcomed relief from the personal authority conflict.

Birth Spacing

Why do these authority conflicts between siblings occur?

Part of it results from birth spacing. If siblings are one year apart, parents can expect more authority conflicts than if the siblings are spaced two years apart. If parents have three children spaced one year apart, there is no peace for mother during preschool years or at least until two of the children are in school.

If children are spaced at least three years apart, a mother has a better chance to train a child and to give adequate attention to each child. For the first three years each child requires a lot of attention. They can play together and enjoy each other much better with a three year interval between births.

If you already have children, this at least will give you some understanding of why quarreling relationships erupt between siblings, especially between the ages of two to eleven years of age.

A major reason for the quarreling is that parents don't understand authority relationships, nor do they know how to teach or correct conflicting relationships. A parent may act as a referee, ignore the situation, or express emotional outbursts thinking that this will correct the situation between the children. These are ways of solving a quarrel. But, without explaining the conflict to the children, it is sure to happen again. The children will not understand how to resolve the conflict unless the parent labels what has happened.

Quarreling (Misuse of Personal Authority)

Labeling Conflicts
"Having an authority conflict again, Bill?" Mother says calmly. "What is the rule?" Mother asks. She reminds Bill about sharing.

Bill reports, "But he didn't ask me if he could play with my truck."

Mother turns to Don. "What should you have done to avoid this authority conflict?"

Don replies, "I should have asked Bill if I could play with his personal property."

"And did you?"

"No."

"Why not?"

"Oh, he wasn't using it."

"Were you playing trucks and cars together?"

"No. He was playing all by himself."

"What should you have done to avoid this authority conflict between you and your brother?"

"Ask him if I could please borrow his truck."

If mother had angrily stopped the two boys or ignored the quarrel, both boys would not have realized why they had a conflict over property rights and authority.

Children need their parents to analyze a conflict like this. Labeling the source of the conflict will help children resolve their quarreling, which may be due to one or more of the following:

> A lack of emotional control,
> A conflict over property or personal rights,
> A misinterpretation of another child's rights.

Rules & Routines

Mothers have all discovered that when pre-schoolers are playing together, usually two can get along better than three. When there are more than three children of pre-school age, a parent must watch them constantly. She can then intervene frequently either to prevent quarrels from erupting or to analyze a conflict so that the children can solve or avoid the situation in the future.

If mother wants peace of mind when two or more children over four years of age are playing together, she needs to establish rules before they play. The children then know the limitations of their personal authority and grow to cooperate with each other. They then learn that making rules for a situation is a peaceful way of relating as human beings.

Rules and routines are ways for children to learn the limitations of personal authority. It is by learning to accept a limitation of one's personal authority by the use of rules and routines that one can have fun.

Children will, in time, learn the necessity of choosing an umpire, judge, or referee when interacting in an activity, particularly if it is a conflict activity such as sports. They will then, when playing basketball, elect their own referee. This is considered a necessity as there are children who will

Quarreling (Misuse of Personal Authority)

take unfair advantage or will not play according to the rules of the game. The umpire or referee limits the players' personal authority, as he interprets the rules of the game. He is there to resolve conflicts.

Taking Advantage Of Another

Children have to be taught not to take advantage of another child or person even though this is natural for a child or an adult to do. Some children will frequently lie, cheat, steal, fudge, threaten, deceive, pressure, form alliances to win, scheme, or manipulate to take advantage of a situation to win.

Mother unknowingly, and through necessity, has had to let her baby take advantage of her. Baby does not know this, but in time he grows old enough to know it. This is probably when quarreling really begins. Mother, as she becomes aware that her child is taking unfair advantage of her or another child or person, tries to stop him. This is when she finds herself in a quarreling situation.

If society is to be improved, it will be with small groups of children, ages four to ten, not at the university level. The art of learning to live like civilized human beings is learned in small groups at this age.

Most children will learn, through the years of growing up, that they must surrender some of their personal authority to have peace, harmony, and enjoyment.

Respect For Privacy

Mothers must, at times, interfere in quarrels of their children not only to prevent physical harm and to stop the noise, but to be sure that the children learn the principles of respect for privacy of another.

If siblings have separate rooms, they will undoubtedly be in each other's room uninvited. When the four-year-old wants privacy, how does he keep the two-year-old, who doesn't understand privacy, from entering his room? Many rooms don't have locks on the doors. In this situation, the cheapest solution is a hook on the bedroom door so that the two-year-old can't reach it.

Older children should knock on the door and ask if they can come in. Every child has a right to privacy.

Many children talk to me in my office about a sibling they cannot restrain from entering their room and disturbing them. A solution to this situation is for that child to walk out of the room immediately if the sibling has not knocked on the door or been invited in. It is an inconvenience for the child to leave his room. It is also an inconvenience to have an annoying intruder.

Going to bed at night can be a quarreling affair when children are one or two years apart and, more so, if they share the same room. One of many mechanical solutions is to have the younger child go to bed at least a half hour before an older child. It gives the older child a feeling of seniority. He feels more like controlling himself when he receives seniority privileges. The younger child looks forward to having these privileges when he gets older. It also compensates the older child for the attention and special consideration that the younger child receives on certain occasions.

A parent should respect the property rights of a child. Frequently a distracted mother, to have peace of mind, will let a younger child play with a toy in the room of another older sibling without the permission of that child. Sometimes something gets broken, moved, or lost and obviously the absent child becomes disturbed when he discovers this.

Quarreling (Misuse of Personal Authority)

He then quarrels with the other child. He also quarrels with mother for allowing his property to be used without permission while he was away. Many times a lost or broken object is neither restored nor is an apology made for the missing or broken item. This can lead to retaliation or hard feelings.

Parents should resist the temptation to loan what is the possession of another child when that child is not at home. This is a violation of a child's property rights.

Years ago I made a small work bench for one of my boys. I taught him he could use my tools if he asked permission and returned them to their place.

One day I was in a hurry and grabbed a hammer from his work bench. He was standing nearby. I started to hammer with his hammer.

"Dad, did you ask me if you could use my hammer?" he asked.

Surprised, I answered, "No. Please may I use your hammer, son?" I asked, remembering that was the fair thing to do.

"Yes," he said, "but be sure you return it to its place." I had forgotten to respect his property rights and my own son reminded me.

Name Calling Doesn't Work

Misusing personal property rights and being inconsiderate usually leads to quarreling.

One of my clients, Mike, age twelve, had a younger brother of eight who was always calling him names. I solved this quarreling situation by having the older brother insist that the younger brother repeat the cuss word one hundred time or if the younger brother would not repeat the cuss word 100 times, he would have to stay in his room without TV for an evening, enforceable, of course, with his parent's permission.

It worked. The younger brother soon learned that "sticks and stones may break my bones, but words can never harm me." He knew that every time he cussed his brother, he would have to repeat the cuss word one hundred time or be grounded to his room without TV for an evening. Amazingly, when the brother had hit the younger brother at different times for calling him names, it was ineffective. Repeating a swear word 100 times or being grounded for an evening, however, was very effective.

Proper Use Of Personal Authority

It is important that an older child not substitute his personal authority for parental authority when relating to a younger child who will naturally retort, "You are not my parent." A parent frequently reminds the older child that he is not his brother's parent. "I am the parent, not you."

Confusing Issues

A parent, sometimes, finds himself or herself in a quarreling relationship with a child and does not know how it happened. This happens because the child has learned to confuse issues. The child will usually put the parent on the defensive by misusing authority relationships. He will assume the parent role and the parent becomes the bad child. The parent winds up accounting for his or her actions to the child. This can happen easily if the parent doesn't understand how to use parental authority. This child is an expert at using excuses and self-pity. He so confuses the quarrel that

Quarreling (Misuse of Personal Authority)

after a period of time neither the parent nor the child remembers what they were quarreling about.

The bully, being an inconsiderate person, always uses his personal authority to make another child feel helpless. He does not respect the personal authority or the personal property rights of another child. No wonder the picked-on child feels helpless.

Quarreling usually means that one of the parties feels helpless and sometimes both of them feel helpless as there is a misuse of authority and lack of consideration.

Helpless feelings come from not being able to correct what seems to be an unfair situation. Quarreling results from one, if not both, persons not making the other quarreler see the unfairness of his position.

The misuse of personal authority is based on being inconsiderate, not caring about another's feelings, rights, or authority. Why is personal authority so badly misused?

Lack Of Consideration

Laws, rules, and routines are generated by the thousands each year to control the misuse of personal authority and the lack of consideration on the part of every human being.

For years, the child's helplessness will control parents, siblings, teachers, and others who are concerned with his care. Especially the pre-schooler, many times, mistakenly thinks his helplessness is real authority and that the world revolves around him. He can't understand why others help him nor does he ever wonder why others help him. They help him because they care about him and want to protect him from harm, either mentally or physically. Lacking the ability to reason, to any extent, until about five years old, the child makes constant foolish demands upon all.

I had a child in my office tell me, "I hate my mother. She doesn't do anything for me."

I asked her, "Who washed your pretty blue dress, Claire?"

"Oh, Mother did."

"Who cooks supper for you at night?"

"My Mother does."

"Well, can you tell me who cleans the house, shops for food and snacks, and plans the activities for your family?"

"My Mother. You are being silly, Dr. Wise."

"Oh, how am I being silly?"

"You know Mother has to do those things for me. She's my Mother and that's her job."

"Don't you think that your mother wants to do something else other than to please her family?"

"Oh, no. Moms have to do those things."

"This is where you are mistaken, Claire. Your mother does not have to do any of the things I have just mentioned, if she doesn't want to. Your mother does all of those nice things for you and for your brother and for your father because she cares about you and the rest of the family. She wants you to have all the opportunities available to you that she can."

"But when I ask her to buy me candy, she always says no."

Quarreling (Misuse of Personal Authority)

"That is because candy is not very good for your teeth. Can you tell me what candy has in it that is not good for your teeth?"

"Oh, sure. Sugar."

"Your mother many times will not buy you candy because she cares for you and is concerned about your health."

"Oh, Dr. Wise, you make Mother sound like she can do no wrong. She is always telling me what to do when I am doing something else. And when I ask her to do something for me, she is always too busy to do what I want. This makes me mad."

Claire's problem was that her mother did not teach her how to use personal authority in a considerate manner. She was still misusing personal authority like a baby — disturbing her mother whenever she wanted something that struck her fancy. Claire felt put upon when her mother used her personal authority to request Claire to do something. In order for her mother to get Claire to obey her, she was forced to use parental authority, which made her seem like a bad mother all the time.

Claire's mother did not gradually set limits on Claire's demands. Claire was not dethroned. She was still the "little queen" and demanded everyone obey her every wish. In Claire's mind, if her mother didn't respond to her demands, her mother was not worthy of her love. Claire was saying that if you do as I say, I will love you, but if you don't, I won't.

If Claire's mother had only known about the five authority relationships and the P.A.L.E. system, she could have taught her daughter to be a loving child.

The Considerate Use Of Authority

When does a parent start to teach a child the considerate use of authority?

How does a mother teach her child to request a need, a wish, or service of another in a considerate manner?

How does a child respond to another person's personal authority, demands, or requests without quarreling or having constant disagreements?

When does consideration of another person really begin?

Parents start to teach the considerate use of authority with **courtesy words and courtesy phrases.** Courteous phrases are the verbal starting point for the considerate use of authority.

Courtesy shows and develops appreciation for another human being. Courtesy habits are also reciprocal and must be learned.

Chapter 10

Habits Of Courtesy

Limited Authority

Courtesy words create respect and remind us that when another person says 'please,' he is telling us that he understands his authority is limited.

Very early parents teach baby the limitations of his personal authority by responding to baby's demands with smiles of approval or frowns of disapproval or just letting baby cry. Baby soon learns to limit his abusive use of authority.

Certainly, when the child learns "no" he is not only learning the limits of his personal authority, but is learning to tell others the limits of their personal authority, too.

Demands Of The Pre-Schooler

I want!

Give me!

Go away!

I won't!

These are the demands every parent hears daily from pre-schoolers and children. They all express the same thought, "You owe me something. You have to do what I want." It is true that mother performs all kinds of services for infant and baby to be sure he survives. After age four, these services change.

The Dethroning Process

The "tip" that every member of the family wants is appreciation. This is the "glue" that binds each member of the family together. There are many elements in the expression of love. One of them is appreciation.

As soon as a child can say "please" and "thank you," he should be made to use these courteous words when and where they are appropriate. This is where courtesy habits begin. Mother begins by smiling, along with a pleasant tone of voice, as she teaches these two courtesies of appreciation. In the beginning, this is a mechanical relationship as baby doesn't have the logic or experience to understand adult reasoning for pressing appreciation. This is why parents should make teaching courtesy fun and say something to the effect, "We say thank you for ..., Please may I have more ..., etc."

With these gentle remarks made by mom, the child eventually gets the idea on how to ask for something in a courteous manner, instead of demanding his needs.

Some children will not want to repeat "please" or "thank you." In that case, after the parent puts the child on notice enough times, mother tells him, "No courtesy, no favor." The child then gets the idea that he better preface his demands with "please may I have ..." or "thank you for ..." whether he understands the courtesy or not. This is the beginning of dethroning the child. It forces him to take the first step forward in becoming an appreciative and eventually an independent individual.

Why Teach Courtesy Habits

Note that at two and three years old the child will forget to use courtesies after being told many times. This is okay for the time being as it is a parent's job, with a smile, to teach courtesy habits in a pleasant way.

Therefore, at first, a parent should expect to remind the child by saying, "Is that the courteous thing to say?" or "Is that the way you ask?" Remember, it takes time for courtesy habits to become instilled in the child's subconscious mind.

Habits Of Courtesy

As courtesy habits are formed, these expressions will pop out of the child's mouth at the right time and surprisingly with affection. This is one of the rewards parents will receive for teaching courtesy habits and for being patient until the child solidifies them.

By the time the child is four, he will forget less and remember more and more to use courtesies; that is, "Mom, please get me ...., Thank you for ..., etc."

If, however, parents do not continue to teach and keep expanding the child's courtesies, when appropriate, then each year after age five, the child, more than likely, will revert to baby habits as he has no direction from the parent. Parents must help the child understand that he no longer has baby rights to expect free service. Parents need to continue the dethroning process or the child will increasingly feel unappreciative toward parents, siblings, and other persons each year as he approaches eighteen.

An example of why courtesies are necessary in the family is indicated by the following altercation between mother and Jimmy:

"You are mean," he says to his mother, when she asks him to come in for dinner as he is having such a good time playing with the friend he hadn't seen in a long time.

Jimmy expressed his feeling openly to his mother. He expressed his dislike of what his parent asked him to do by reverting back to baby thinking. His retaliation was based on, "I want my own way, and if I can't have it, you are mean."

For years, mother had allowed Jimmy to be nasty to her, while still performing services for him. She, unfortunately, did not dethrone Jimmy. He never gave up his baby habits.

101

The Road To Appreciation

Appreciation is a major reason for teaching courtesies to a child from the time he can say, "thank you."

After a child reaches age five, parents do not respond to the demand, "I want." They only respond when he says, "Please, may I." Then the child recognizes the authority of the parent by asking permission, not demanding it. These authority courtesies are taught to break infantile habits of thoughtlessness — only thinking of his needs and not the needs or feelings of another.

The parent gradually nudges the child to express courtesies with an affectionate and a positive attitude, not in a rote or mechanical way as he has done in the past.

When a child makes a request, this is the opportunity for the parent to change baby expectations of free service to a realistic understanding of a relationship. The parent says to the child, "Do I have to do this for you?" A child will naturally be puzzled by the statement. The parent then explains to him, "You are no longer a baby. You can do this for yourself. I no longer need to do this for you. You are no longer helpless. True?" The child not wanting to be a baby, sees the logic of these statements will answer, "True."

Mother further explains by asking, "Why should I do this for you?" The child, again puzzled, has no answer as mother had always done this for him in the past. The parent answers, "I do this because I love you and care for you. So tell me, what do you say when mother or anyone else does something for you?" From years of rote training he should say, "Thank you."

In time, he will learn that courtesies are a way for him to change from thinking solely of his personal needs to thinking of the needs of others. It is the parent's job to get this idea across to the child. Through courtesies, he learns appreciation and respect for others. Without courtesies, he can develop self-pity, which is based on, "You owe me."

Courtesies teach a positive way of living. They are called the sweeteners of personal relationships. More can be won with affection than with a negative tongue. Sweet words should flow from the mouths of babes and adults. By not teaching courtesies is to encourage selfishness — a disregard for the rights of another human being.

Building Courtesy Habits

Between the ages of six and seven mother helps her child gradually make the transition from being the center of his universe to recognizing the rights of another. This transition doesn't happen overnight, but as mother repeats phrases of appreciation, eventually the child catches on how to appreciate another person. Mother may start by asking the questions she has already given him the answers to.

"Will you be happy if I do this for you?"

The child eventually answers, "Yes."

"Then how do you express your appreciation?"

"I say, 'Thank you.' I know you don't owe me this service. I appreciate that you care for me."

This answer from the child may take several years to accomplish. The parent continues to build habits of courtesies by asking the child questions until he reaches adulthood.

"Why do you say please?"

The learned response should be: "Whenever I ask a favor, I use a 'courtesy' to remind me and to let that person know I have no right to expect anything from him."

'Thank you' is a courtesy phrase that shows appreciation for a favor done, or about to be done.

'Please' is a courtesy word when asking permission to boss another person. It is to remind one of his limited authority and that he is asking a favor.

Gradually, through the years until eighteen, the child increasingly uses the courtesies "thank you, excuse me, please, etc." At first, these expressions are mechanical, rote, and perhaps thought silly, but as the child reaches out to others by using courtesies, he becomes a sincere and an effective communicator. He then begins to understand why courtesies are important.

No doubt the child will experience rude treatment from children who never made the transition out of baby behavior and are still the center of their universe. This contrast between courteous and rude behavior is evident. Rude human behavior is the teacher for all to understand the necessity of courtesies. Such rudeness is expressed by children ridiculing one another for their size, weight, lunch box, clothes, etc.

A System Of Courtesies

In order to make the five authority relationships effective, there must be a system of courtesies. Therefore, every child must be taught habits of courtesies by their parents in order to develop worthwhile feelings of oneself as well as towards another human being. Courtesy habits produce feelings of self-respect in an individual, and are reciprocal, benefiting both parties.

Parents must gradually help the child put away the **demanding gifts** he was born with to survive — **Give me. I need. I want.** These demands of the infant are no longer needed for survival. The parents must replace these demands by teaching a system of courtesies. This includes limiting the child's authority in order for the child to develop love, respect, consideration, and appreciation for another. It goes something like this:

"I know and understand the limits of my authority, and I realize that another person has just as much authority as I have. Through courtesies — I will develop respect, love, consideration, and appreciation of another human being."

Courtesies are expressed with respect. So we address a letter, **"Dear Sir," "Dear Madam,"** or **"Gentlemen,"** which is an affectionate concern for another person.

A **"gentle"** woman or man is one who respects another and who knows how to use courtesies and how to express them constantly.

Courtesies In Use

Courtesies are the great protector of property, personal, and political rights. Courtesies are being considerate of another's personal and property rights. Parents must teach courtesies to their children. Children who are not taught courtesies may invade another person's privacy or property.

There are neighborhood children who will enter a neighbor's home, without knocking on the door. The courtesy system starts at home and it naturally gets extended to individuals outside the home. Up to seven years of age, adults can excuse children for a breach of courtesy on the basis of ignorance or inconsistencies. After that age a child should be held accountable and should suffer the consequences for a **breach of courtesy.**

Children after age five should be taught to knock on the door of their parent's bedroom for permission to enter if the door is closed. This is their private room. Children should also be taught to respect the privacy of a sibling by knocking on the door of the bedroom before entering and saying, "May I please come in to visit?"

At the dinner table when the food is passed, it is proper to say, "Thank you." Food in the refrigerator does not belong to the child, but to the parents. So a child asks, "Please may I get a drink?" or "Please may I get an apple from the refrigerator?" The child who is taught to ask for food instead of just taking it will probably not have a weight problem. He learns self-restraint and consideration of other members in the family.

Asking permission to use a toy, to enter a room, to go into the refrigerator, to go outside after supper, to go over to a friend's house, etc., is part of the courtesy system parents need to teach children.

Correcting A Mistake

Saying "I am sorry." is an important expression for a child to master. At first, the phrase is learned as a rote expression to correct a mistake of the three-year-old by saying that he is sorry. When the child passes the age of five, the parent expects an extended explanation of this expression. A parent will ask for an explanation many times over the years until he is assured the child truly understands why he is using this courtesy.

Habits Of Courtesy

"Sorry" is a word of consideration, expressing an awareness that another person's feelings may have been hurt or that his property may have been damaged. When causing an inconvenience to another, this word is used.

"Sorry" can restore feelings that have been hurt. The child who is aware quickly makes amends for hurt feelings by saying, "I am sorry." If the child is never taught to say, "I am sorry," he remains ignorant of this expression. He may also wonder why the hurt individual remains cool and aloof.

It is the admission of a mistake and the willingness to correct a mistake that counts. It is important to admit a mistake so that further damage or trouble can be averted. To ignore that you have troubled another person is diminishing that person's self-worth and injuring the relationship.

Correcting A Violation Of Rights

"Excuse me" is another important expression to master if you walk in front of someone. You are telling the person that you have no right to walk in front of him and would he please excuse the disturbance you have caused him. With this, the person forgives that person for walking in front of him. Otherwise, by rights, the person gets hurt feelings and may think or say, "Who do you think you are walking in front of me like that?" It is a sign of ignorance, inconsideration, and selfishness to violate a person's rights without an "Excuse me. Pardon me. Please forgive me. I didn't mean to do that. Won't you accept my apology?" etc. These words create goodwill and good feelings toward the violated individual.

Group Acceptance

Learning to say "hello" is important as it establishes the person as being friendly and approachable. Immediately identifying yourself and giving some biographical information aids another child or adult in communicating with you. Saying "hello" to playmates on the playground is important as your child is recognizing the importance of all the playmates he is playing with.

Many children enter a classroom or playground ignoring the other children and speaking only to special friends. I have known teachers and parents who are oblivious to this kind of single-minded behavior. Acknowledging others by saying "hello" is a way of teaching equality and making the other children feel accepted in the group.

Many parents allow their children to come to the breakfast table without a word. No cheery "good morning" but sad, stone faces surround the breakfast table. Some families don't even bother to sit together to have breakfast before starting the day. These families have few enjoyable hours to share from morning to evening.

Many of these children may grow up depressed because they did not learn appreciation and respect. They never had much fun sharing. Plus, what is there to look forward to if you have no feelings toward family members or your fellow man. Many parents fail to teach their children consideration, by not teaching courtesies. Every person in the family deserves a cheery, "Good morning. Was your night restful?" "Thank you for asking."

It is the obligation of every person to make himself happy. Granted, in one's baby days, mother took the responsibility for cheering up baby with a big smile and "That's my big girl, wide-eyed this bright sunny day. We must get you washed and dressed to meet the flowers and the sunshine." No spouse, child, or adult ought to expect another person to

Habits Of Courtesy

make them enjoy living. **By the time the child is nine, he should have been taught courtesies**, which not only make him happy, under normal circumstances, but other persons and animals as well.

Party & Social Courtesies

Courtesies are also for parties and social occasions as well, so no one will be treated unfairly. If everyone is affectionate, good humored and obeys courtesies, most everyone will enjoy the occasion. It is built into the courtesy system to spread cheer and not to make another person unhappy, particularly at the dinner table, social occasions, or parties.

If children are not taught party courtesies before they go to a party at four, five, six, or seven, they will not know how to relate to other children and perhaps stand there not saying a word. But if the child is taught the courtesy of extending a hand with a smile and immediately saying "hello," he will have a great time at parties and other social occasions.

If a child also beams a big smile as he or she leaves a party or social occasion and says, "I had a great time. I am so glad you invited me," this child will never lack for friends or invitations to social occasions.

To help one's five- or six-year-old avoid awkward social situations where he and others are meeting for the first time, you teach him to say "hello" first. He gives his name and then asks the other child his or her name. Then he makes comments about something; such as, "I am five years old. My birthday is next month. I have two rabbits at home." He then has relieved himself and the other child of an awkward situation. Your child, if he learns this social grace, will never be without friends.

Looking Into The Eyes

You tell your child to look into your eyes when you speak to him or when he speaks to you. In this way, he learns the courtesy due any human being when speaking to another.

When your child greets or talks to people outside the family, he will already have the experience of looking into the eyes of family members when he says "Hello. Excuse me. Thank you." He will see delight, sadness, anger, disappointment, whatever is reflected in the eyes of another.

If the child doesn't look another child in the eyes, he will miss clues that will tell him how to react to that child or adult. **If you train your child to watch for the clues in the body, eyes, and words, he will communicate more easily with another.**

A child who has received a lot of disapproval and whose conversations are ignored may be shy and may avoid looking another person in the eyes. This child expects to read disapproval in another person's eyes. As he grows older, he may overcome this fear of looking into another person's eyes or this may persist for years.

The Word "Polite"

When a child asks his parent the question, "Why do I have to say 'please' and 'thank you'?" Many parents reply, "That is being polite, Dear." None of this can be expressed to a child by saying, "It is polite. That is why we do it."

This is true, but after talking to hundreds of children, I find that ninety-five percent of them do not know what the word "polite" means. The word "polite" is not a motivator nor an adequate explanation. None of this can be expressed to a child by saying, "It is polite. That is why we do it."

Children need an explanation as to why courtesies are

used. By explaining the system of courtesies and why we use them and how they originated is a much more satisfactory answer, instead of just telling them, "You do it because it is polite." There is a lot more for the child to know.

The King's Court

Courtesy words express the "civil" or "personal" rights of every human being. Point out to your child the small word "court" in the word "courtesy." Explain to him that this refers to the king's court. He was the authority and he insisted that every person who came into his courtyard or room behave in a certain way, indicating that his subjects understood and respected his power and authority. The subjects, in seeking the king's favor, were very careful to be obedient subjects. In no way did they want to act in such a way that would offend the king.

The king appointed judges to make decisions for him to keep peace in the community. When attorneys, clients, witnesses, or spectators came into the court of the judge, they all used certain manners, which came to be called "courtesies." Everyone in the room had to perform these courtesies to show respect to the judge, the king's representative.

To show disrespect to the judge was considered a disrespect to the king himself. Disrespect was not tolerated. **The acts of respect are called courtesies.**

This is still true in the courts of the United States today and in the courts of other nations. Any public official must be treated with respect even though this is a democracy.

These acts are to remind the persons in court that the judge doesn't have to please them since he has the power to order their execution, fine them heavily, or throw them in jail should he choose. An individual had better be careful to use his words carefully so as not to offend or displease the judge, the king's representative.

Every person has authority and can do favors. Every citizen in a democracy is equal in this respect. Therefore, every person must respect the other person's authority and vice versa. So one is expected to say "please" and "thank you" when a courtesy is due another.

Paying Tribute To God

Among Christians everyone is considered important to God. So if any person who is Christian fails to acknowledge the importance of his fellow man, he is dishonoring God. Since the commandment is "to love one another," then it's more important for a Christian parent to teach the worth of another by saying — Please. Thank you. Excuse me.

For centuries, children were taught to say "yes, sir" and "no, sir" out of respect for adults. This was motivated for religious reasons as well as for reasons of the king's court. It was also part of the class system of the 1700's and the 1800's.

Immigrants Effected Courtesies

During the colonial days from Portland, Maine, to Atlanta, Georgia, the king's subjects were wondering what to do with the English courtesy system. Some parents were teaching their children not to say "sir" and "madam." There was a question as to whether titles should be used. Some wanted to abolish courtesies all together.

Those who didn't understand the difference between formal occasions and informal occasions thought courtesies that applied to formal situations also had to be applied to informal situations. They too, not understanding, rebelled

Habits Of Courtesy

against using all manners, thinking that the manners of high society were some form of snobbery. They were partly right. They were also partly wrong.

As the stream of immigrants came to the United States, the standards of courtesies were affected. In the Southern States, the courtesies of England were maintained and are still encouraged today. Yet, it was a Virginian, Thomas Jefferson, who may have cut the root of courtesy when he expressed that "all men are created equal."

Since courtesies of that day had their roots in the King's court and his Judge's court, there were Democrats who wanted to destroy the courtesy system as they thought it reeked with class structure which they thought destroyed the dignity of the human being. There was little question that some of the courtesies were built on "I am superior to you" and were constructed to keep a certain strata of human beings in their lower place. What these men forgot was that the same system kept a so-called higher class person from abusing the lower class person.

Telephone Courtesies

The telephone is an interesting mechanical device for a three-year-old who cannot understand, "How come I hear grandmother's voice when I put my ear here, mommy?"

My wife, while running her publishing company, would set our baby boy, Franklin, in his portable chair which titled backwards on her desk in the office while making sales contacts and company calls. She would say, "Good morning. This is Joyce Wise from the Wise Publishing Company ..." and she would take orders and say, "20 *BEES*, 15 *TEE PEES* ...*etc.*" Franklin, of course, watched her while drinking his bottle. She never realized he was self-learning by listening to her introduction and taking orders on the phone.

One of the first things Franklin wanted to do as soon as he could was pick up the receiver and listen. We knew he wanted to do this because he held out his little hand and would say, "a-a-a-h, a-a-a-h," when any person talked over the telephone. So that day we held the receiver close to his ear and saw his eyes grow wide as he smiled, especially when he heard his grandmother's voice.

By the time Franklin was talking, he had heard grandmother's, grandfather's, and my voice on the phone many times. One day the phone rang and Franklin surprised us by running to answer it saying, "Hello, This is Franklin David Wise. Who is this speaking?" Both my wife and I looked at each other as if to say, "You did a good job getting the courtesy lesson across to him." But later when we compared notes; neither of us had prompted him on what to say.

It remained a mystery until about a week later when Franklin again answered the telephone and said, "Hello, this is Franklin David Wise. Who is speaking? Oh, Nana. Wait Nana," he told her, as he pulled a piece of paper from the telephone pad and picked up the pencil next to the phone, "Okay, 2, 4, 7, 6, 10… I got it" and hung up. He turned and walked away from the telephone without a word to either of us with a look of contentment and went about playing with his cars just as though nothing happened. It then occurred to us how he figured out all by himself how to answer the phone. He had watched my wife talking on the phone first introducing herself and then taking orders.

Children learn by imitation so be sure your courtesies are worth imitating. You never now what your child will copy.

Chapter 11

Manners
(Home, Company & Public)

Home Manners vs. Company Manners

"Your Bob was so well-behaved when he stayed over-night with our Jimmy," says Jimmy's mother. Bob's mother replies, "I am so glad to hear that. I wish he would be that way at home."

When parents hear this report about their children, they are puzzled. They wonder why is their child's company and public manners better than their child's home manners?

Parents usually brief their children on how to act at a friend's home. Some parents don't need to say anything. They can rely on the child's training and his natural good conduct. When children are guests, they know if they can't control themselves, they may not be invited back. Children want the visitation rights to continue, so they behave.

Three to six year olds usually lack the foresight or belief to understand that they might not be invited back, so they fail many times to control themselves. At this age, parents expect to watch, control, and forgive their misdeeds.

Away from home a child knows that teachers, friends, and strangers owe him nothing. So, he knows that he has to act differently than he does at home. He is told rather rudely, at times, by non-family members how to control himself.

Many times when parents do not teach manners, it is because they take the love of their children for granted. Therefore, they do not see the necessity for insisting on manners at home. But manners must be taught at home so that peace and harmony prevail. It is just as important for children to express appreciation at home as it is in public.

Unfortunately, many parents who are well-mannered themselves fail to teach the child manners in an affectionate way, but only as a perfunctory duty. They may also not think it important at this time. It is no wonder then that a child's home manners are, at times, very different from his company or public manners.

Why Must Manners Be Taught?

Teaching manners must be taught for an important psychological change to occur between the ages of four to seven.

The parent helps the child make the transition from demanding to developing appreciation and gratitude for what is done for him. Manners are a way of making this transition happen.

Acquiring Appreciation & Gratitude

From birth until three years of age, a mother does not mind if her baby takes advantage of her. Mother loves these years even though her child makes demands upon her. Parents naturally assume their children love them and appreciate everything that is done for them. This obviously is not so since children, from the beginning, take most things for granted and even think that their parents owe them all things.

A child may get angry and demand what is thought to be rightfully his. Many times a child will express displeasure instead of appreciation over a gift or over an outing.

To acquire appreciation and gratitude towards parents, or any human being, a child must be taught the fundamental principles of etiquette. A primary principle of etiquette is — no one owes you anything. When a child understands this principle, then appreciation and gratitude can grow. The thought that no one owes you anything ends demanding.

Manners (Home, Company & Public)

Daily living can then become a rich experience, instead of a series of frustrations and disappointments.

To help the child make the transition from taking loving services for granted, to appreciating services rendered, the parent asks the child between the ages of five to seven (when appropriate), "Do I have to do that for you? Do I owe you this service?"

The answer should come back, "No."

"Why?" asks the parent.

"I get what I need because you love me," the child answers, "not because I demand it or want it."

These statements must be asked many times until a parent observes that true appreciation has developed. When the parent thinks that the transition from baby demands to appreciation has occurred, the questions need no longer be asked.

I will frequently ask a child or teenager the following questions in my office to see if this transition has occurred:

"Did your mother or father show you love today?"

The usual answer is "No, they did not."

"Who made your breakfast and prepared your lunch?"

"My mother."

"Why did she do that for you?"

"Because she is my mother. She has to feed me."

"Oh, she owes you that?"

"Yes."

These are the usual answers. After having talked with many children over the years, I am not at all surprised at some of the answers I get.

I ask these questions as a way of helping the child understand that their parents do love them and that their parents do have rights just as they do. So I tell them.

"No, mother doesn't owe you that service. She cooks for you out of love. She cleans house out of love. Mother does many things for the family to make you comfortable, feel clean and adequate. She does not owe you any of this. She gives to you out of love."

Development Of Mature Love

For the child to think his parent does not owe him anything is a stunning thought for the child, as it destroys the "baby concept" of love. Baby love is taking, not recognizing another person's needs. Baby expresses appreciation with a hug, a smile, or a kiss. It gets very tiresome though to have a seven-year-old demand baby service, or for that matter, a four-year-old. Therefore, as soon as the child is ready to do a thing on his own, the change must take place What the child must learn for a true relationship to take place is to know and to understand that mature love is a give and take relationship. Appreciation is involved.

Probing the child with additional questions, my intent is to destroy the concept of baby love and to develop an appreciation for the parents' love. Hopefully, this will further develop the idea of what mature love is in the teenager and the child.

"Does your mother wash your clothes?"

"Yes."

"Why does she do that?"

"She is my mother. She has to do that."

You would think after asking the question previously that by now the child would know the answer, but he doesn't.

"No, she does that because she loves you." I tell the child.

If it is a teenager, I want him to get the idea that it is time for him to take care of himself. In a few years, he will be an adult. This is also another form of mature love, not putting unnecessary loads on those who love you.

"Are you able to wash your clothes?"

"Yes. Why do you ask?"

"Because at your age, I think that you ought to be washing your own clothes, folding, and hanging them up. You ought to start taking care of yourself. Do you at least hang your clothes for your mother?"

"Oh, no. That's too much trouble."

Obviously, from this comment of the teenager, "baby love" is deeply entrenched. Taking care of oneself is a stunning and an objectionable thought for many teenagers.

A parent should expect that as soon as a child is able to take care of himself, he should be expected to do so. As soon as a child can dress himself, he does so. As soon as a child can tie a bow knot on his shoe laces, he should be expected to do so, etc. This will cause a child to be appreciative if the feeling relationship between child

119

and parents is excellent. Otherwise, there will be anger and resentment because the child must take care of himself.

Now I continue my conversation with the child to get him to recognize fatherly love.

"What about your dad?"

"Oh, he just goes to work everyday. He didn't do anything for me today."

"Why does he go to work?"

"Oh, he likes to work."

For some men this is true. Work may be more important than their family and the family is just a show piece. But there are many men who work because they want the members of their family to have it better than they did as children. Thus, check out the following:

"So, he didn't show you in any way that he loved you today?"

"No way."

"If your father didn't work, how do you think he would pay for the house you live in, your meals, clothing and entertainment?"

"I don't know."

Again, he thought that everything was owed to him by his father, as he had thought of his mother.

Creating Appreciation

Children are really bewildered by father's expression of love. The daily disappearance of father is difficult for pre-schoolers to understand. This causes an alienation between father and child. If the father's habit is to bring a surprise home for the youngster, this is appreciated by the child as is the rough housing. Many times it seems as though father is buying love, which is not true, as far as father is concerned. He wants his child to be happy and this seems to him like such an easy way to make a daughter or son happy.

Mothers, who do not frequently explain father's love to the children nor does she express her appreciation of him in the children's presence, creates without knowing it, an alienation of feelings between father and children.

Appreciation takes on new meaning when parents teach that neither one of them owe the child anything, but they are giving things to the child out of love. In addition to this, it does prevent alienation between parent and child or child and child. **Appreciation creates strong, affectionate ties.**

It is also important for both parents to teach their child to express gratitude to the other parent if they want to increase their love for one another.

If father takes the children to a movie, mother teaches the child or children to express gratitude by saying, "Does father have to take us to the movies?"

"No, mother."

"Why is he taking us?"

"Because he loves us and wants us to have fun."

"If father buys drinks and popcorn, why does he do that?"

"Because he loves us and wants us to feel happy."

"So how do you show appreciation for his love?"

"We thank him and tell him we love him."

When the family sits down for dinner, father teaches the child or children to express gratitude to mother by asking, "Was this a good dinner?"

The children chorus, "Oh, yes."

He then asks them, "Why did mother spend so much time preparing the meal for us?"

"Because she loves us."

The children then say, "Thank you mother for the good dinner. We love you."

If both parents do this often enough, children will finally come to understand that parents don't owe them anything and will express gratitude, appreciation, and affection towards their parents and siblings.

Husbands and wives sometimes, too, forget that neither of them have a right to expect or to make demands on the other. Spouses do not owe each other anything. A spouse gives to the other because he, or she, wants to and feels as though they should because of loving concern.

Parents should remind children often that gifts, services, etc., are not owed, but are given out of love. These reminders to children also remind them that they do not owe each other anything. This should increase marital as well as family affection.

Love Grows Displaying Manners

Even though no one owes any person anything, laws are made and must be kept. Laws are made to force everyone to keep them even though the individual may not know the law exists. Ignorance of the law is no excuse. For example, a person didn't agree to pay a certain percentage of taxes, but he will. He owes it.

Manners (Home, Company & Public)

A man and a woman who are well-trained in courtesies before marriage can expect a more affectionate and respectful relationship from each other and their children. The wife and husband who are just as loving, but didn't have the benefits of courtesy training as children, should have more difficulties with each other and their children, as they don't express appreciation often enough to each other.

Manners are a way of teaching a child how to love, not only in a general affectionate sense, but in the petty details of human interactions. In fact, the more petty details that are correctly expressed through consideration and cooperation, the more an affectionate relationship increases.

Adult love grows by mastering expressions of affection through manners — the petty details of human interactions.

Name Calling

Name calling is destructive to any person. It attacks the worth of another individual. Parents do it to children. Children, in turn, do it to parents. Siblings to siblings. Children think that they have a right to tell another child — "I hate you. I don't like you. You are a dirty woo-woo. You are shrimpy. You are too fat. Hey, skinny." This is not an appropriate way of relating to anyone or to correct a mistake. In fact, this is considered "bad manners."

It takes a lot of habit training to teach the child to disapprove of an "action" and not of the "person." A child is always a good person, he just makes mistakes for whatever reason. The point is to correct the mistake, not condemn the child or person.

Name calling is tactless. Tact is a great smoother of human interactions. Knowing how to make corrective statements without hurting the worth of another person is one of the necessary skills for anyone who desires affectionate relationships.

Petty Details Of Living

One important petty detail for parents to explain to children is if a member of the family leaves the house, someone in the family should know where he will be. This is just one of the principles of being concerned about another person and helps to make the family feel secure. It is an act of adult love.

Another petty detail as far as fathers are concerned is the time children spend talking on the phone. Fathers need to explain to children that they can only talk a certain amount of time or the privilege will be taken away for a week.

Mothers, however, are more concerned about children interrupting her conversations. Mother needs to explain that children are not to interrupt her while she is on the phone or there will be a consequence. Any child seven years of age or older can always write a note to mother if there is something important she needs to know.

Very likely it was the petty courtesies that turned many adults off to rules of conduct. Perhaps they didn't see, or were not taught, the importance of learning petty courtesies as children. Petty courtesies lead to affectionate relationships.

Many persons, unfortunately, take petty courtesies as courtesies owed them. They get insulted when a person fails to perform petty courtesies. Other persons have abandoned petty courtesies as a way of avoiding bad feelings that come from such confrontations. This, too, is just as serious an error.

Manners (Home, Company & Public)

Formal events, particularly a dinner, a wedding, or a military parade are filled with petty details. One must be trained as a child to accept and appreciate the pettiness of formal expressions of human relationships.

It is easy to dismiss formalities because one is ignorant of the petty details which makes one feel inferior and awkward.

There are important days during the year that give members of the family special ways to express their joy and love for each other. These events are most important in creating loyalty and devotion. These family events are expressing love in the general sense, not in the petty sense. Still, if an event is to be successful, petty details need to be taken care of to make the event an emotional success.

Birthdays

Every member in the family has a birthday. This can be celebrated by giving gifts and having a party, or by just sending a card. It is a day when all try to express their appreciation that the person was born. On that day, too, the birthday child ought to feel lucky to be born into an affectionate family.

To create mutual appreciation, a child on his birthday should probably celebrate by having a present for his parents to express that he is glad that he was born and glad that he has parents and siblings. To neither have a present for the parent, nor to express appreciation for their care since his birth, is to continue baby love and baby expectations.

The Wedding Anniversary

It is important for the whole family to celebrate the wedding anniversary as it is the continuation of generations of the family. Children express their joy that mother and dad found each other. They all express their happiness over the founding of the family. In the case of the divorced family, the anniversary date is lost and forgotten.

House Entertainment

There are moments when guests, children, or adults are invited to the home for whatever reason. It is important for children to have friends to dinner and to spend the night or to visit the house for entertainment. This is how a child learns that a house is not just a place to eat, sleep, and quarrel, but that a house is a place to learn the art of being a host or hostess. Moreover, the child learns that his friends are important to the members of his family, as well. To entertain is to teach the child how to express friendship.

Religious Events & Holidays

Christian families have additional family events that non-Christian families do not have. There are manners of conduct practiced in connection with these events. Not only to increase appreciation for each other within the family, but to every human being on earth. Christians express appreciation for God's love which increases their consideration and affection for each other. So they say grace at meals and family prayers.

To express the fact that they belong to the same family, the family of Christ, they call one another brother and sister. Having had a spiritual rebirth signified by baptism, they are born into this larger Christian family.

In Christian families there are the Christian holidays and days of significance such as christenings and baptisms. Christmas and Easter are celebrated in the home to acknowledge the joy that the family has experienced through Jesus. It is the acknowledgment of their common joy in sharing Christian love with one another. Sundays are enjoyed at church sharing the love of other Christians which strengthens the ties of the family, the ties between families of a particular church, and the ties of national and world fellowship.

In Jewish families their religious holidays are really celebrated more so in the home than in the temple. The Jewish family also feels that they belong to a larger Jewish family group, that of the temple group and the international expression of their faith and culture.

The democratic expression of the appreciation of all religious faiths is based upon the constitutional right of any person to worship God in his own way. There is no superior religion according to the laws of The United States.

Good manners then require that each citizen respects another citizen's religious convictions.

The School & Social Systems

The public school assists family living. Teachers are teaching manners every day. Parents are so concerned with the child learning the three R's that teachers are not given credit for teaching manners as well. It is the failure of parents to teach their children the manners of daily living that makes it difficult for teachers to accomplish more.

The school provides a structured way of living. Teachers do teach children to live by rules and routines. Teachers expect children to be able to boss themselves on the basis of rules and routines. They expect students to be obedient. Rules and routines are the means whereby groups can live and cooperate with each other. Teachers also teach national courtesies, such as national holidays, patriotic anthems, respect for The United States flag, and many other courtesies.

Formal and Informal Events

There are formal rules for social situations that the older child is expected to know. Many children will balk at almost any new experience they must learn. Formal rules are to protect the worth of everyone involved, to ensure fair treatment to all. They also ensure, if possible, that everyone has a joyous occasion. It also gives every person an excited feeling by seeing the beauty and dignity of the formal occasion.

A parade is a formal occasion and the pinnacle expression of the formal.

There are the national holidays to celebrate so that all can express their appreciation of the sacrifices made by others in order to have personal benefits; such as liberty and the pursuit of happiness, equal opportunity, the abolition of discriminations, freedom of expressions, and many other wonderful values.

A child should appreciate the formal as well as the informal occasion. Not only is the child enriched, but the family and the community as well. Formal and informal occasions require lengthy explanations by parents and adults to children so that they know how to act and how to appreciate these occasions.

Manners sweeten every human relationship. Therefore, manners will always exist. Those who practice them will always be called "gentle" women and "gentle" men.

Chapter 12

Feelings

Happy Faces, Sad Faces & Stern Faces

Being wanted and admired makes life worth living. The newborn who feels unwanted will quit nursing. When the baby loses too much weight, the doctor puts him in the hospital and prescribes tender loving care from a nurse. Affectionate nurses then love the baby into eating again. Positive feelings make life worth living.

After the umbilical cord has been cut, the baby begins feeling hunger pains. Baby now experiences both positive and negative feelings — happy faces and sad faces, not only in connection with eating but with many other experiences in adjusting to a new environment. Any of these adjustments cause either sad or happy faces.

Mother necessarily has to wait for baby to cry to know what to do. This develops in a few weeks into a knowledgeable language for baby and mother. A pattern is set. Baby learns to make himself unhappy, and gets tender loving care. There will be milk and dry diapers. There will be cooing and talking with a caring mother who rapidly responds to baby's needs. Baby gradually develops a feeling of self-confidence and power.

With an unresponsive mother, crying and more crying leaves the baby feeling helpless, defeated, and very unhappy —"a thumb sucker."

Poor health from date of birth sets a pattern of more sad faces than happy ones. This may last a lifetime even though mother is loving. The power of emotional control is learned in a matter of days after birth. All that is needed to make feelings more powerful are the addition of words. Sometimes the helplessness of a baby is more powerful than words.

The Power Of Feelings

Feelings have great bargaining power. Mother can bribe with a smile. She can threaten with an unhappy face. Distracting or withdrawing attention can be a powerful weapon that a mother can use for bargaining with baby. She also has a pleasant or an unfriendly tone of voice that she can use.

As mother uses her feelings this way, she will, in time, teach baby unintentionally how to control her by the same feeling tactics. What baby experiences, baby repeats. Baby discovers accidentally, in the early weeks of life, how to control parents with feelings.

It doesn't take too much intelligence to discover the power of feelings. The mentally retarded baby responds to positive and negative feelings. Animals of all types respond to feelings.

Every adult carries an image of what a mother ought to be like from the early months as a baby — she is tireless and totally devoted. She is always available to take care of baby's slightest whim. Fun loving, too. The purveyor of delicious food. Always available. Super person. She has no needs. Takes nasty treatment with a smile. She's never cross. She's perfect. More divine than the angels.

What happens to this loving mother's image after the first twelve months?

As soon as baby learns to walk, mother baffles her pre-schooler as she switches rapidly back and forth from the loving mother to the restricting mother many times during the day. She becomes more baffling as the child's language develops. Now mother is not only more restrictive, but makes baby start to take care of himself. "Oh, whatever happened to my Garden of Eden?" thinks the preschooler after age three.

Feelings

Thus, every pre-schooler develops ambivalent feelings towards mother. Every mother needs to be aware that during the day she will evoke not only the loving image, but the unloving image as a habit trainer. The child will carry these contradictory feelings and images for years.

The child, in turn, expresses ambivalent feelings towards every member of the family as well as persons outside the family. If angry feelings are successful, the child continues to use these. If sweet feelings are successful, then the child charms his or her way through life.

By knowing that the reaction of "mean mother" may develop in her child's mind because she is a habit trainer, she can help her child to overcome negative responses to her training methods.

The Real Mom

What might mother really be like? She can be a scared teenager who wishes that she had never gotten pregnant. She could resent her husband. She could have ill health. She could always be tired, crabby, and doesn't do any more for her baby than is essential. She may not be too well-informed. Has little interest in developing parental skills. She can be drug addicted or alcoholic or a junk food addict, or all three. Some mothers give their baby away. Thousands of babies are destroyed by abortion. There are a variety of mothers

Most men carry the image of the happy face, tender loving mother of baby days in their subconscious minds when dating, not the images of a variety of mothers ranging from happy to sad, or from super to terrible. The dating experience for men and women may be an unconscious revival of these feelings of the early months of a baby. The Garden of Eden is discovered once again.

This unconscious image of "supermom" which the baby has during the first eighteen months may cause men to pick the wrong women to marry. They think that this image of "supermom" is natural to women. If men didn't have this image and other misconceptions about women, there might be fewer men marrying the wrong women and vice versa. Fewer babies might be born if men knew that there were such a variety of mothers.

This image of "supermom" probably keeps every adult from insisting on parenting courses for men and women. Men seem to think that women are born with the knowledge of how to rear children. Many men certainly don't want to rear them. They just want to create them. They want to be a proud father at the expense of mother's efforts.

If men were really interested in rearing the child, they too would take courses in parenting. If men had enough parenting knowledge, they would either marry women who wanted to be mothers or refrain from creating children.

The Christian Madonna

The Roman Catholic and Greek Orthodox Christians hold up to every Christian the image of the Madonna as an example of what a woman ought to be like. This is still considered by the Christian community an excellent image for women.

Expecting to be like a Madonna, however, may keep women from expressing their true feelings about being a mother. Mothers are not allowed to say that they don't like the responsibility of parenting. Until recently they were not allowed to even say that they didn't want to get pregnant. They had no choice, that is, until birth control came on the

Feelings

scene, right after World War II, when contraception was discovered and became available.

Baby's Effect On Parents

Every baby automatically learns to emotionally disturb parents to survive. Baby learns that by crying, being angry or sad gets results even from a mother who doesn't care. Sad faces and happy faces motivate mother. Every child knows the truth of these statements. The seeds of emotional instability rests in this statement. If a mother can't create more happy faces each day than sad faces on her child, she feels defeated. Her husband will criticize her. The psychotherapist is hopefully called to make the baby "feel better."

Feelings Of Unhappiness

One of the unfortunate ways of training a baby, or a child, is to make him feel unhappy when he has done something wrong. The belief is that this will cause a correction of the wrong act. Sometimes this is effective, but not often. If this training is maintained long enough, it may cause the child to become neurotic.

Frequently, one result of correcting by making the child feel unhappy is that the child thinks the parent does not like him. Another response may be, "I am scared." The feeling response can be, "Why try?" Another one might be, "I like suffering." or "I'll suffer before I give in."

Children who have been trained this way will also try to make another child feel unhappy when he does something wrong. This can confuse the other child if the child was not taught to feel badly but was trained to change his behavior to remedy the wrong.

Creating unhappy feelings within oneself or within another person is certainly not the best method of correcting wrong interactions between persons and their wrong actions.

Mistakes Need To Be Dealt With

Before two years of age, the child usually isn't aware that he has done anything wrong. From two until age four, the child doesn't have enough self-control to keep from making frequent mistakes after being corrected. Instant learning is not characteristic of the human being.

Anger, belittling, sarcasm, name calling, frightening, and hitting are not necessary to correct a mistake. Any of these tactics may work temporarily. What is needed at this time is a calm approach, along with patience and understanding in handling the mistake and preserving a person's self-esteem.

From birth to six, the parent is steadily teaching a child not to make himself unhappy when a mistake is made; that is, not to be sad, not to be angry, not to hit, not to spit, not to name call, not to cry, not to sulk, etc. Since it is natural for the human being to make himself unhappy to get what he wants, it takes quite a bit of parenting skill to correct a mistake.

A step for parents to take when a learning mistake has been made is to teach the child to have a happy face, not a sad one. The parent points out to the child that everyone makes mistakes when learning something for the first time. The trick is to catch the mistake that has been made and to assure the child that it can be corrected with practice. What is important is not the mistake, but correcting it with practicing doing it right, not giving up or feeling inferior.

A parent will usually correct a child for destroying property, for disobedience, for lying, for failure to carry out chores, but will, many times, neglect to correct the feelings involved. As long as the child doesn't repeat the error again,

Feelings

the parent, sometimes dismisses the action and neglects to recognize the importance of correcting the feelings involved.

Correct Feeling Relationships
Parents have to correct feeling relationships as they do for all other kinds of wrong relationships, such as cheating, hitting, stealing, etc.

A child can be forced to do what is required of him daily for years, but he can be harboring resentments that affect his relationships with other human beings, his successes at school and at play activities. If the child harbors such resentments, he may count the days until he is an adult and can do as he pleases. The successful performances of the child fool the parent into thinking that he has accepted correction for his mistakes without feelings of resentment. Unless the feelings toward the parent or teacher are corrected, too, little of the training he received will be effective.

Correcting Jealousy
If jealousy is displayed and not corrected, it can cause the child no end of unhappiness. Jealousy keeps a child in a constant state of despair as it rests on how the child perceives himself or how others perceive him. He constantly compares himself to others which makes him feel threatened. When parents witness this trait in their child, they should compensate and try to build the child's self-worth which will help get jealousy corrected.

Anger (A Cry For Help)
Temper is an emotion that definitely must be corrected particularly when property is destroyed or another person is struck.

What causes anger?

It is a helpless feeling that erupts into loud noises. It is a demand for help. The person is saying, "If you do not help me out of this situation, I'll scream at you. If you meet my anger with anger and not help me, I'll hit you."

If it is treated by the other person to whom the anger is directed as a threat to his well-being and not recognized as a cry for help, there will be a fight. The person frightened by anger does not realize that the person screaming is feeling helpless. The anger does not sound like helplessness, but it is.

What Makes Anger Seem Like Strength?

The strength of the anger is in the belief that another person can help or solve the problem. The forgotten feelings of baby days, "You are my mommy. You have to and will help me." is the expectation of the infant and later the expectation of the adult.

A person who is frustrated by a wrong and becomes angry tries to solve his frustration either by blasting the other person with verbal vituperation or by beating him in an attempt to get the wrong corrected. He feels helpless in correcting the situation. "Yell loud enough and somebody will come to rescue me."

Recognize that when you see this type of anger, it is a cry for help. Unfortunately, children mimic their parents who act this way.

It is important to teach a child to say, "I feel very helpless. Can you help me?" instead of letting the child express anger at the parent, another child, or teacher. Sometimes this feeling of helplessness is the fault of the parent. The child has tried to get the attention of the parent, but couldn't. The child needs an answer from the parent, but feeling helpless by the parent's indifference, the child screams at the parent.

Feelings

Anger can be based on self-confidence, on moral certitude and sometimes on physical strength. This is righteous indignation.

Problem Suffering vs. Problem Solving

Many parents teach children "problem suffering" not "problem solving." This is a serous misuse of emotions. Anger is a case of problem suffering. This is why anger must be corrected. Suffering will usually not solve the problem.

Suffering did at one time solve difficulties for everyone. When one is under two years of age, mother solves baby's difficulties when baby is suffering. Why? Because baby is helpless and the solutions are usually easy: milk, diaper, holding, tickling, distracting, etc. This is registered in the subconscious mind of everyone that suffering can solve difficulties.

This is the gambling approach to human interactions. "Maybe someone will answer my 'problem suffering' like my mother or dad did," thinks the sufferer. Sometimes another person does feel sorry for that person and solves his difficulty.

When wrong solutions are tried by a child, perhaps once out of fifteen times, the child will luck out and solve it. Problem suffering will work once in awhile. Most of the time, individuals get wise to the problem sufferer and avoid him.

Many children suffer internally as they are afraid to tell their parents what their difficulty is for various reasons. They are afraid to ask or talk because the parents' frequent reply is, "You're old enough to solve that," or "I'm too busy to be bothered by that," or "Why do you let that bother you?" The reply may be, "talk to me later," and later never comes.

The parent makes remarks while talking to another

person about how dumb someone was in handling a situation. The child overhearing the comment figures, "The only answer I'll get is, "How could you be so dumb?" So the child spends a lifetime suffering, rather than asking or telling anyone about his personal difficulties. Many times the problem may have been solved by just stating the difficulties to another person.

Many mothers and fathers think that as long as they are adequate maintenance parents, this is all that is required. Beyond that they think that a child should be able, after six, to manage his own affairs.

In fact, this is considered a way of helping the child to be independent, by forcing him to solve his problems the best way he knows how. These parents may be overreacting to the over-solicitous parent who responds so readily to every whimper.

Feelings Of Inferiority

Everyone overlooks the fact that a child is born with an inferiority complex. For three years everyone is taller, can walk faster, and talk better. In fact, for months, a baby can't understand any of the sounds. These are painful feelings. It isn't until a child is a first-grader that he can begin to feel superior.

A child has to be trained out of an inferiority complex. The inferiority is real, not imaginary, up until six years of age. The baby can't talk, walk, or feed himself. As baby learns to walk, he stumbles, falls, trips, feels stupid and is called clumsy by other children.

Constantly, until six years of age, the child hears, "You're too little." "You are just a baby." Little wonder that every person has inferiority feelings and low self-esteem at times.

Feelings

In later years, inferiority can be imaginary. Even for children of various ages, an inferior feeling can be based on imagination.

Fear springs from an inferior feeling. "I can't do it because I'm too little," says the child instead of saying, "I'm afraid." Children have found that this response can get them out of more emotional difficulties. No wonder the child prefers problem suffering to problem solving.

Since many parents don't know how to solve human relation difficulties, how can they teach their child to face difficulties without fear? Parents, however, do solve many difficulties in spite of their fears originating from unsolved inferiorities.

A parent always needs to be praising, reassuring, patient, and supportive of the child. Parents also need to know that it takes years to overcome countless actual inferiorities.

Imaginary inferiorities are more difficult to overcome than real inferiorities. A person can see and feel real inferiorities. There are several ways to train a person out of real inferiorities.

However, imaginary inferiorities are very real to that person but there is no way that one can be trained out of these by usual methods. This is why inferiorities are so difficult to correct.

A child lives with helplessness based on inferiorities and parental restrictions for years. This engenders all kinds of fears. Parents must be aware of what the years of helplessness will do to a child.

Feelings Are More Powerful Than Logic

The management of feelings can determine if a child is strong, self-confident, self-assured, or able to overcome difficulties. It also determines if a child is fearful, indecisive, hesitant and inferior. Thus, the management of feelings is not stressed enough. **Nothing except hunger and thirst are more important than feelings.**

Good feelings rests on a strong body, an adequate diet and plenty of athletic activities. The weakening effects of sugar, soft drinks, and junk food are not properly credited by parents as causing the negative feelings of their children. They can sometimes see that these foods and drinks do affect the physical health, but they fail to see that it affects feelings and the emotional health of the body.

Logic and feelings are connected as both track over the same neurological system and both are coordinated through the brain. Feelings can be overwhelming to a person without the benefit of logic. Logic can overwhelm feelings to the point that a person can't properly relate to either human beings or animals.

If there is not a loving, feeling relationship between parent and child, or adult to adult, any type of logical solutions may not work.

Years ago I worked as a director of craft activities and was also a cabin counselor to a group of boys at Camp Lanakila in Vermont. One of my boys, age eleven, who slept in the cabin was the son of a famous man in the Senate of the United States of that era. Elmer was homesick and anxiety ridden. He could not wait for the four week camp break when campers were permitted to go home. These boys were signed up to stay for eight weeks.

I did everything possible to make Elmer happy, but at the beginning of the third week, I saw that I had failed as had the other staff members. The camp was in a beautiful setting and had a great program, but nothing was pleasing this

Feelings

boy. I finally realized that kindness, concern and affection on my part was just failing. During an after-lunch recess period of an hour, I took Elmer for a long walk. I told him that I thought he was not grateful. I also told him that he was not appreciative of all the fun things he could do at camp. I told him that I thought something was disturbing him.

With this comment, Elmer broke down and admitted to me that he was not thinking about camp. I was right. There was something disturbing him. His teacher had given him an impossible reading assignment for the summer. He wanted to get home for that. He thought that his parents didn't love him and that he had been sent to camp to get rid of him. Out tumbled all his sad, anxious feelings. I knew then why we had not succeeded.

After our conversation and a couple of telephone calls, he became happy. He stayed for the following four weeks and a post session of two weeks.

Feelings can be and usually are more powerful than logic, particularly if those feelings are "fear originated" as in the case of Elmer.

Misinterpretation Of Faces

I have seen many children in my office who hate loving their parents. The parents have been so kind and understanding that the son or daughter does not understand the relationship between them and their parents.

Many of these children feel unloved and express their bitterness, resentment, and unhappiness in my office. It is because of these feelings that they plan to run away from home. A parent can be so understanding that sometimes a child misunderstands.

Remember the unreasonable expectations of early baby days. Baby is a great misinterpreter of love. If this misinter-

141

pretation is not corrected, the relationship between parent and child can grow increasingly difficult during the years that a child lives at home.

If the feeling relations are superior, then almost any solution will work. Any couple madly in love will live in the most difficult conditions, and enjoy it.

To help a child develop good feelings every day, a parent can make a happiness chart if the child is having unhappy relationships. This is a way of correcting misinterpretations.

On a sheet of paper, the week can be marked off into days. Each day the child can have happy faces for happy relationships. Sad faces for unhappy experiences. At the end of each day, the child can see if there were more happy faces than sad ones. Parent and child can now sit down and talk about how he got a sad face and find a solution so there will not be another sad face.

This is a way of teaching emotional control. If a day later the child solves the situation that created a sad face, then he can erase the sad face. As the sad face situation is solved, the sad faces can be redrawn into happy ones.

The point to be made is that as long as a child continues to incorrectly relate, there can only be sad faces. The moment though he can change an unhappy interaction into a happy occasion, unhappy memories are forgotten. So the child can redraw the unhappy face on the chart to a happy face. If the situation is really difficult and unhappy, the parent can offer a reward for a happy face.

The fact is that feeling relationships are being considered and dealt with. The by-product is that- the child feels he counts and it makes for a closer relationship with parents.

PART IV - DEVELOPING SELF-MANAGEMENT

Chapter 13

A Consistency Chart

Consistency requires involvement by memorizing tasks and/or activities correctly. The result of consistency is self-control and automatic behavior of a habit.

Inconsistencies Lead To Deceit

"John, have you fed your rabbits? This is the fourth time I asked you this morning," yelled John's mother. "Do I have to get rid of them? What will it take to teach you to care for the rabbits you love?"

Then comes all the excuses and alibis John learned over the years to disobey both the personal and the parental authority of his parents. His parents lived with his excuses and alibis for years. It was the excuses and alibis that allowed John to escape from being responsible for his actions.

This morning will be no different, and John knows it. His parents will not hit him, nor will they sell his rabbits. They will just continue to get upset, which John doesn't mind. He will continue to be irresponsible and act like a three- or four-year-old child until he is forced to mature. John, now fourteen, doesn't know that he has not matured. He doesn't know that he is still thinking like a baby.

After all, John drinks, smokes pot, swears, and has sexual intercourse with his fourteen-year-old girl friend. He is an adult now. Isn't he? All this, of course, his parents do not know. John's parents taught him well how to be deceitful. They would deny this, and rightfully so.

By accepting John's inconsistencies and excuses, his parents did not teach him the necessary self-control to mature. By accepting John's alibis, they did not change his baby misconceptions about daily living.

If inconsistencies and excuses are the source of trouble between parent and child, then how does a parent avoid a situation like John's?

Shifting Responsibilities

The answer may be a consistency chart. This training device is for both parent and child. Both parent and child usually have to be trained to use it. There are mothers who don't need the chart for themselves, but need it for their children.

The consistency chart is not new, just the title. The title, however, is important. It tells both parent and child what is important in human relations — self-control and consistency.

To make the chart effective, the parent must become a habit trainer and know how to teach a system of habits. The chart shifts the responsibility for the child's actions from the parent to the child. The child trains himself to acquire a system of habits to accomplish a task. The chart is a method of self-training and develops regularity. If a habit is going to be permanent, the child repeats all the steps over and over again until the habit becomes automatic. The habit must enter the subconscious mind to become an automatic act.

At What Age Do You Use A Chart?

With some children at age five. With most children, after they have entered the first grade.

The Consistency Chart

At what age do you stop using the chart? Usually until about age ten. It really depends upon the child.

How long does a parent use charts with a child? Until the child masters enough essential habits and accepts being responsible for his actions. How soon the child accepts the shift of responsibility from parent to child, or teacher to child, depends upon the child.

Forming Habits

The child must recognize that unless he practices an idea and commits it to memory, it is valueless. The idea must be important enough in the child's mind so that he will desire to commit the idea to memory to form the habit. Then the child must repeat, repeat, and repeat the idea until the subconscious mind accepts the idea permanently. The child must develop pride in himself so that he does not wait to be reminded by an adult, as only babies and small children wait to be reminded. The purpose of the consistency chart is self-bossing to escape being "parent" managed.

Making & Using The Chart

A parent makes a chart by choosing several tasks for the child to perform — not more than four at a time. She takes a sheet of paper and lists the four tasks. She marks the chart off into seven days with blanks to be checked. She places the chart on the child's bedroom door or bathroom mirror, or on the refrigerator door — any place where the child can't fail to see it. Attach a pencil to a string so that the child cannot use the excuse, "I couldn't find a pencil."

After the task is done, the child makes a check mark on the chart for that day — not the parent. If the mother marks the chart, then she is assuming the responsibility for getting the job done — not the child. Self-learning can't take place this way. There must be a shift of responsibility.

Now if the child is really irresponsible, a parent may need to use bribery until he develops some sense of responsibility. With six-year-olds, you can say to them, "You will get a dime a day if you check and perform these four tasks. You will have to wait until the end of the week though before you can collect your money."

Then place seven dimes in a dish on the dining table at the beginning of the week. In this way the child can see what he, or she will get at the end of the week. Each day that the chart is not checked, the child loses a dime. This hurts. You can win and lose immediately. The child requires an immediate reward and punishment.

The Power Of The Subconscious Mind

How long do you continue with the chart?

Probably three weeks and in some cases nine weeks. It depends upon how much the child is motivated. Some children accept responsibility easily, but do not grasp the point that regularity is important. Once the child grasps the idea of consistency and learns to use the power of the subconscious mind to help him, he becomes consistent and develops consistent habits faster.

But, if the parents believe in the magic of words, and do not insist on following through, it takes the child much longer to catch on to consistent habits. So to help the parents follow through, the dimes in the dish are there to remind them to follow through. The chart is there to force parents to quit relying on words as if they were a magic wand. Words are worthless without the habit to accompany the words. If the child has a baby habit of not doing what is asked of him, he will not see the value of doing what is necessary. The

The Consistency Chart

parents must break the baby habit that they were forced to nourish by the very nature of a baby.

The parents may have to be gently forcible at first. Dimes may not be enough to break a six- or seven-year-old habit of not responding to directions. The chart is there to break two sets of bad habits — parents' and child's. It will not be easy for either of them. The parents may want to quit first. Unfortunately, parents and child, will pay a price. The price is quarreling, disappointment, and aggravation for years to come. Mother and father will also see their child fail because he can't boss himself well enough to succeed at school, in youth organizations, and with friends.

Using a chart with rewards causes immediate changes in bad habits. The parents can then accept the disturbances that accompany breaking a bad habit. Plan on six weeks of difficult relationships. The parents must remember that they have been having difficult days for months or years and that they learned how to accept suffering and defeat.

The child thought he was winning, but he, too, learned to accept suffering to win. Suffering has become a way of life for the family. Now is the time to change it.

Setting Goals & Measuring Progress

By the second or third chart, bribery should not have to be used to get the child to accept a system of habits. Wisdom, the feelings of self-mastery, and better human relationships are more satisfactory to a child than some types of material rewards.

Years ago, I was explaining this chart system to a group of women in Hollywood when an elderly lady from the audience stood up and said, "Dr. Wise's chart works for husbands, too. I would keep asking my husband to do necessary chores around the house and in the yard. For some reason my requests were almost always forgotten. Then one day I put the list of requests on a chart with target dates. From then on my husband took care of the necessary maintenance of house and yard."

This kind of scheduling is done in industry and schools. The form may be altered for different situations, but the idea is the same. One needs to set goals and measure daily progress.

A consistency chart is setting goals and measuring daily or weekly progress. Scouting sets goals for children to achieve. The 4-H Club does the same. Vacation Bible Schools have set goals and offered rewards to the children for remembering so many Bible verses or whatever the teachers have thought desirable to learn.

All nature seems to be set on a reward and punishment system. Either work according to natural laws of human beings or get hurt. There is no escaping this system.

Charting may finally force this conclusion upon a child's consciousness. Do it right and reap the benefits. Do it wrong and all kinds of difficulties seem to happen.

Charts Develop Consistent Habits

There are all kinds of schedules for self-control. This is just one that presents the fundamentals of all scheduling — consistency. Doing a thing day after day regardless of how one feels, with no excuses, develops reliability and dependability.

The Consistency Chart

Charting can be a cure for negative feelings. Negative feelings hinder self-mastery. The charts help a child and parent to discover feelings as well as the excuses that prevent him from doing what must and should be done.

Excuses are meant to defeat a parent. Excuses work because a parent usually wants to avoid confrontation or the parent believes in the magic wand — power of words. The parent wants to preserve the image of not being mean. He or she may want to avoid being like their parents, who were believed to have done a poor job of parenting.

Charting teaches a child not to use excuses or feelings as a way of getting out of what must be done regularly.

Illness may prevent a child from having regular habits. Allergies and asthma certainly interfere in the habit training of the child. The child feels cranky, tired, irritable, and not caring. It is tiring to be consistent when fighting your body.

Some children though seem to achieve beyond their limits and who knows why.

I remember a child who had performed on a radio program that I produced for the Scouts in Wichita Falls, Texas. He had a cleft palate and stumps for feet. This child could do amazing things.

There was a fourteen-year-old boy who was referred to me because he liked to watch women undressing through windows of homes. He also had a pornography problem and would stop at a magazine stand and thumb through pages of magazines looking for nude women. During the first appointments, he kept his left hand in his pocket. As we talked, I was amazed as he told me he played golf, basketball, and baseball, all of which he did well. Why was I amazed? His parents had told me that he was missing his left hand.

149

Children and teenagers have taught me that no one has an excuse for not becoming responsible for their actions. So while parents make allowances for illnesses, they should do it only to a limited extent. Don't let the child out of anything that he can do. A parent may just slow down the time it takes for self-mastery. Parents should not be defeated by the child's disability nor allow the child to be easily defeated.

Children with ill health need a consistency chart even more than a well child. They need the encouragement of success that a chart can demonstrate. Hundreds of children have improved themselves through charts.

Sometimes the difficulties are so severe that a parent will need professional help to correct bad habits such as bed wetting, sleep walking, thumb sucking, sugar addiction, disobedience, etc.

If the charts don't work, you may need some coaching to be a parent, or your child will need professional help.

Nursery, kindergarten, or grade school teachers may know that your child needs professional help, but will not volunteer the suggestion unless they see that you will act on it.

Charting is an excellent way to acquire essential habits of self-management.

Chapter 14

Clubs Teach Children
Self-Management

The Turning Point

It is a big day when a boy or a girl goes to nursery school, kindergarten, or first grade. The child is so unaware of what it will mean to him or her in the future. For a parent, it is the turning point in training a child in self-management. The parent is now forced to share the training in self-management with others until graduation from high school. The teachers will be busy teaching children all kinds of generalizations to help them live in an industrialized and technological society. They will also teach all kinds of skills. How well teachers succeed, depends upon how well parents have taught the framework of self-management at home.

For the hours after school, there are a variety of children's organizations. These clubs are necessary for children to join. They are important as children learn many of the elements of self-management, not taught at home. Adults, who have had club experience as children, will testify to the value of these organizations.

If a parent hasn't trained the child properly in the preschool years, then it is questionable as to how much training in self-management a child will accept from these organizations. One may also wonder how cooperative the child will be with the leadership.

If, however, the child will cooperate and is willing to follow club leadership, even though he wasn't taught much self-management as a pre-schooler, these organizations can be of great help in developing self-management in this child.

151

How much a parent participates wholeheartedly in these clubs will determine how much a child will improve.

In the Boy Scouts, the parents should be prepared to read the manuals, buy the necessary equipment, encourage regular attendance, talk to adult leaders, and/or invite some members of the den or patrol to the house. There is always help needed for transporting scouts.

This is also true of church organizations, 4-H Clubs, and other youth organizations. Remember the leadership consists of volunteers.

The Need For Clubs

What brought about the need of clubs for children?

Increased personal wealth, increased leisure time activities, and most of all the change from farm life to city life. Now that mothers work, the high divorce rate, and the increased use of drugs by children make clubs even more necessary.

Prior to the 1900's most of the youth organizations did not exist in rural United States.

Children from age six to twelve living on farms prior to 1920 seemed to grow up more quickly than children living in the city. They usually learned sooner how not to be "mother" managed. They seemed to have a more meaningful existence than most children living in the city. Farm children more readily gave up dependent ways.

There were things to see and do. There were chickens to feed, cows to milk, sheep to shear, butter to churn, etc. Work was never done. There were adult activities that the child could participate in and perform.

A child looked at the sun, like an adult, to measure time. He looked at the skies to see if it was going to rain. He

Clubs Teach Children Self-Management

watched the winds and the clouds as the adult did to see if the snow or rain was going to fall. **There were adult conversations to hear. Listening taught the child common sense.**

They walked, ran, rode bikes, and horses. They were active. They spoke to everyone.

The adult skills necessary to survive in a farming civilization were easy to acquire. By sixteen, many teenagers were working full time and many girls married at that age.

Then came the big change, following World War II.

Today the nation's population exceeds three hundred million citizens, most of whom live in twenty-five large cities instead of farms and small towns. Group action and group living is important today. No one can escape the organizational community.

Changes In The Community

Since 1940, due to the movement of population from the farms and small towns, the biggest change for the child from six to twelve years of age is the small backyard. This hinders the child's development of self-management. What can a child do in a small backyard? There are no more vacant lots in many sections of the city.

With the invention of TV, the technology age of computers, cell phones, iPads, video books, etc., the living space of the child has shrunk even further to a space of three feet by six feet. To overcome the handicap of the backyard, the loss of the vacant lot, and the disrupted family, adults have been busy since 1900 creating organizations to help the child have fun and to prepare him for adult living.

Athletic Sports

There are all kinds of athletic programs today — organized sports for children of all ages such as T-ball, soccer, Little League or Pop Warner, YMCA and YWCA programs, athletic leagues, summer camps for those interested in sports. There are gym classes, Karate, and swim classes. There is athletic equipment galore available in the sporting good stores.

None of it is of much value, however, if there isn't a parent there to teach a child how to manage himself while doing these sports. Unless a coach or an adult or older child takes time to teach the child the elements of self-management for that particular sport, the child learns little about self-management while engaging in athletic programs. For many children, athletic activities create feelings of inferiority if there isn't a parent there to support the child.

Long before athletic activities came to the fore, one of the earliest youth organizations was the Boy Scouts.

Children's Organizations

Because of Lord Baden-Powell's military experience in Farica, he returned to England to organize the Boy Scouts. He did this partly to prepare boys to protect the British Empire by preparing for military service and partly to develop character and to have fun. Another motive was to develop boys to adjust to the newly emerging industrial age.

The Scouting movement began in the United States with the Boy Scouts. Then, thanks to Harriet Lowe in Savannah, Georgia, the Girl Scouts was organized. In time, the Brownies, the Cubs, and finally the Explorers were organized. Children from eight to eighteen could enroll in the Scouting program. All of these clubs of Scouting were designed to teach the framework of self-management to boys and girls. The Eagle Scout award was the Scouts' finest way of sa-

Clubs Teach Children Self-Management

luting the boy who could organize himself. A boy had learned to manage himself by going through the ranks and accumulating twenty-one merit badges.

As modern agriculture developed, farm leaders saw that children needed education for the new farming life and so organized the 4-H Club.

The 4-H Club has an excellent program for males and females which is directed more to the boys and girls of the rural community than the city community. This program is definitely designed to promote self-management and increase independence.

In England, the Sunday School movement was created to help children. Since then, the leaders of the churches have organized programs from birth to twenty-two years of age to teach self-management and independence.

There are church camps and weekend retreats.

There is the YMCA program.

There is the Sunday school program for children and youth.

There are Boys Clubs of America.

There is no lack of organizations to help a parent overcome the handicap of a small backyard and to help the child spend those seventy-two free hours after school creatively.

Many parents, even though they belonged to these organizations as children, may not really know how to use the framework that these organizations provide to help their child grow in self-management.

Organizations Teach Self-Management

How does a parent use these organizations to help

train a child in self-management? In the early days of clubs, parents were more or less ignored. Lately, this has changed. Most parents do not see these clubs as an extension of parenting.

All of these organizations can and do teach the framework of self-management as I have presented it in this book.

All youth organizations are essentially the same — to develop self-management. All of these organizations will increase the child's independence.

Each of the organizations have adult member officers with delegated authority. These officers delegate authority to adult leaders who in turn teach children and teenagers a framework of self-management. It also teaches children that authority rests with the group and the individual members. These organizations maintain the political ideas of a democracy and to give practical experience to children in making a democratic organization work.

These elected children or teenage leaders have the opportunity to exercise personal authority and delegated authority.

The adult leaders certainly exercise personal authority as well as delegated authority — as a parent, as a sponsoring unit, and as a national organization.

There are rules to guide the members' activities. Some of these rules are drafted by the national organization; some created by adults and leaders; and some by the members themselves.

There is a code of ethics to guide the members every day. There is an advancement program to guide them to increase their self-management and independence. There is a helping hand program. There is a parent involvement program.

The Scouting Movement

The Scouting movement is a national youth organization

Clubs Teach Children Self-Management

that boys and girls have joined by the millions.

The scout leaders are volunteers who probably have no more than four to six hours a week to give the children. He, or she, is usually untrained and may not have been a scout himself, or herself. He, or she, probably has had little or no training in child development or has little or no funds to work with. So be grateful to him, or her, for what they may accomplish.

While the scouting organization has an excellent weekly program, the leaders teach little about authority relationships, although there is an excellent organizational plan for its use. There is, however, an excellent system of delegated authority for boys and adults.

The scout law and oath is the code of ethics that will help the scout learn to control himself if the parents and the scout leadership use it. It is repeated weekly and occasional talks are given about it. These talks are important to an individual scout from time to time.

The scout law and oath are to be used by parents at home when a social situation has been mishandled by the scout or parent. The parent asks the scout which scout law has been broken, or how has the scout oath been disobeyed? Then the scout can see the effectiveness of the scout code. How it could have prevented trouble, if obeyed.

A parent occasionally asks the scout if a good deed has been done, which helps make this helping hand program more effective. The parent participating in this way makes this part of the program effective in teaching self-management to a child.

Ranks and badges further extend a scout's ability not only to take care of himself, but to take care of others as well. Parents need to spend an hour a week with son or daughter developing their scout's interest in terms of the badges and ranks. It is a self-improvement program, but a child can use some parental help in improving himself, or herself.

Scouting gives the scouts an opportunity in bossing others as well as being bossed and to accept being bossed. It certainly gives every scout the opportunity to boss himself on the basis of rules.

The scout should have a time schedule for getting his badges and for his activities completed. He should be saving money for camping and the National Jamboree.

The Cubs and Brownies, a part of the scouting movement, have their code, too. Mother and father can use that code at home.

Parents should expect that their child will spend between one to three hours per week on programs. The programs do not rely on the meetings alone. These programs are designed to use a part of the seventy-two hours of leisure time that every scout has. It also is a big aid to parents in helping their child manage his seventy-two leisure hours.

4-H Clubs

The 4-H Club also has an excellent personal code which parents can effectively use at home. The projects are well supervised. There are the fairs which are a wonderful experience for boys and girls who belong to this club. Parents should encourage their child to spend time each week with their projects. If the member has live animal projects, he will be spending some time every day with the animals. A parent almost has to be a member, too, to make the program effective in the life of the child.

Religious Organizations

Parents fail to use religious organization programs for their child's training in self-management, whether Catholic,

Clubs Teach Children Self-Management

Protestant, or Jewish.

I have never heard a parent (in all my years of working with church youth organizations) ask a child when he has done something wrong, which of the Ten Commandments did he break? In fact, few of the children can recite the Ten Commandments. This is also an excellent code to live by, and I have included a copy of the Ten Commandments at the back of the book.

I seldom hear parents asking children six to twelve years of age, which ideas of Jesus apply to parent/child difficulties such as, "Honor your father and mother." Jesus obeyed his parents "not my will, but your..." The story of the prodigal son, etc. There are many more examples parents could use.

The Survival Of Democracy

A democracy cannot survive without citizens who know how to make a voluntary organization effective. Children's clubs provide this kind of training. The way to make democracy work is by enrolling children in these clubs.

The child needs the encouragement of youth and adult leaders and other children, not just parents. A teacher of two hundred students per day in a junior high cannot give the personal attention to students that a scout leader, a religious leader, or any other youth leader can, over a two- to three-year period of time.

Schools must necessarily have children sit and passively learn. These youth programs give a child the opportunity to exercise what they are learning at school and at home. These are most effective educational programs when properly led and supported by parents.

By taking music lessons a child will gain a lot. Learning to practice at least fifteen minutes a day for the first year is

159

one of the finest training programs for self-mastery there is.

The martial arts are equally splendid in teaching a child how to master not only his body, but to express respect for the other person as well.

Self-management training after age six is a shared responsibility with other adults.

Any association, family, team sport, youth organization depends upon the individuals being able to understand and practice the five authority relationships and all the other elements of the framework of self-management.

When an individual has not learned the elements of self-management properly, a friendship ends, a marriage ends, parent-child relationships fail. In spite of all the changed ways from an agricultural society to an industrialized society to a technological society, managing yourself is no different today than it was one or two hundred years ago.

The framework of self-management will always remain the same, even a hundred years from now.

All the success of any human association for a child depends primarily upon mother, not father, unfortunately. She teaches her child self-management. All of civilization rest on how well a mother can train her child during the pre-school years.

NO ONE IS MORE IMPORTANT THAN A MOTHER.

Chapter 15

Parental Authority

Foundation Of Civilized Societies

One of the most important foundations of a civilized society is found in the effectiveness of social organizations. Social organizations depend upon parents teaching their children that there is a final authority to be obeyed to preserve the peace and cohesion of any group. If parents fail to teach children to obey rules and to follow routines, to be punctual, to pay dues and to fulfill commitments, then social organizations will not function properly.

Organizations delegate authority to individuals in order to function. Parents must teach their children early on to recognize and obey delegated authority. This is a principle of any social organization — obedience to the authority person and obedience to the rules of law.

Obeying Delegated Authority

There are many persons in the community who have delegated authority that must be obeyed. They, too, have personal authority that can be disobeyed. There are always risks when a child or an adult disobeys the personal authority of a person with delegated authority such as a policeman or a teacher.

There are always risks when one disobeys the personal authority of another person — delegated authority or not. Children can forget if the authority person is too friendly and nice that delegated authority, such as, of the policeman, teacher, store owner, employer, umpire or judge all must be obeyed. They are trained to act and to enforce the rules, policies and laws.

Teachers are public officials, charged with keeping the peace at school, not just so that the learning process can take place, but so that the child can learn how to respond to public officials or adults outside the home. Parents and teachers too, at times, forget that teachers are public officials.

Parents are expected to support public officials to keep the peace, but not to support their personal opinions. When they cannot force the child to be obedient to public officials, the child is placed in a juvenile hall or suspended from school, or in rare cases, put in a foster home. The peace and harmony of a group will not be disturbed says the city, state, and federal government. Peace and harmony must first be learned at home if it is to be practiced in public places.

Delinquents, or so-called bad children, have just not been taught authority distinctions by parents or teachers. They have not been taught the limits of their personal authority. They keep pushing their luck. They take advantage of the good nature of an authority person. Consequently, they have trouble with parental, delegated or personal authority. Some become criminals for life.

Civilizations rests not just on a mother's love, but on her ability to teach her child to respect personal and parental authority and her rights as a person.

Limits Of Authority

There are many times when a mother or father must say to a son or daughter, "I am talking to you as a parent." Then the child knows the limits of the child's personal authority. There are limits to everyone's personal authority. A child must learn this truth in order to be happy with himself and others.

Parental Authority

Parents who fail to teach limitation of personal authority to their children are confusing the authority relationships between parent and child and also between teacher and child. This limitation of personal authority should be kept clear in the mind of the child, not only for peace and harmony at home, but for those times when the child is out in public, particularly at school.

Personal vs. Parental Authority

Personal authority is just asking a child to do something. If the child refuses, there is usually no consequence. The request may not be that important to mother. But when a call to come to the dinner table is disobeyed, mother switches to parental authority rapidly. Her attitude becomes serious and the tone of her voice is stern. The child knows he better obey or else.

Parental Authority Bears A Consequence

Mother starts off by using personal authority when calling the family to dinner. If the child does not respond to mother's personal authority, she generally uses parental authority. Sometimes a child is confused as to whether mother is using personal or parental authority.

If the child does not obey after parental authority is expressed, it may be that he has not been taught the seriousness for disobeying parental authority or perhaps he doesn't know the difference between the two authorities. Parental authority must always bear a consequence for the child who disobeys it. The parent then must distinguish enough times between parental and personal authority for the child so that he is aware of the difference. The child can avoid the consequences of disobeying parental authority by obeying.

Not until mother teaches the meaning of parental authority and enforces it can she expect parental authority to be effective with her child.

Understanding Authority

"Come to the table now, Mary, and eat your dinner. If you don't do it this instant, you are in trouble." This and similar commands are recognized by Mary or any child as instructions that better be performed.

If, however, you ask Mary why she obeyed this type of command, she may shrug her shoulders and say, "I don't know."

It is the tone of voice that a parent uses to get the child's attention which gives an urgency to the command. Although the parent does not label it as such for the child, this type of command is parental authority.

If the child fails to respond, the parent needs to frequently ask the child when making such a command, "Am I using parental authority?"

Why ask your child this question?

It is important for the child to understand the difference between personal and parental authority. If the child doesn't understand which authority (parental and personal) the parent is using, he may not obey either type depending upon his mood.

The child is daily experiencing these two types of authorities. Sometimes he adjusts well, while at other times he does not adjust at all.

Considerate vs. Inconsiderate Child

A child who is appreciative and considerate when mother calls him to dinner answers, "I am coming, Mother," or says, "As soon as I wash my hands and face, I will be there." Mother then only has to use a mild type of personal authority to get her child to act and will not have to use parental authority. This is a very pleasant type of interaction between mother and child.

The inconsiderate child, however, forces mother to repeat her instructions many time before he responds to her request. "Come to dinner. Dinner is ready. Please come to dinner before it gets cold." These are the numerous pleas that mother uses. Despite all of mother's pleas or resorting to yelling or anger, the child does not move or answer mother until he is ready.

It's not because mother is a poor cook, she is probably an excellent one. It's not because the child is not hungry, he is just inconsiderate and does not respect parental authority.

The Stubborn Child

With the really stubborn child, mother may have to let the child suffer the pangs of hunger for a meal before he learns his lesson. This is a better approach than anger, scolding, belittling or constantly reminding the child. It is quiet, calm and effective. After such an experience the child will respect mother's parental authority. He either comes when called or he goes without dinner.

The child who failed to respond to parental authority, probably as an adult, will only recognize authority or rules as it suits his convenience.

If mother cannot solve calling father to dinner, her best solution is to get her child to respect her parental authority by coming to the table to begin dinner without father. She gets her child to dinner without upsetting herself. Father eventually may get the idea or mother may have to tolerate father's disrespect for dinner rules without getting upset.

Weakening Of Parental Authority

Many times, father is a frequent offender. He probably did the same thing to his mother, who may have failed to correct him for being inconsiderate and disobedient. He, too, at times, ignores his wife's call for dinner. He is weakening her parental authority as well as his own by his delayed response. By father's actions, he fails to teach their child to be considerate, appreciative, and obedient. He fails to teach what parental authority is and what it means.

Collecting Injustices

By the time mother gets everyone seated, she is completely upset. Who gets blamed? Mother, of course. She is a nag; she's always angry for no reason — so her family tells it.

Then, it's mother's turn to collect her injustices now that everyone is seated at the table. "You do this to me every night." she complains. "I don't feel like eating." She goes on and on throughout the meal telling her family of the aggravation and indigestion she is experiencing because everyone has upset her by not coming when called to dinner.

Does all this complaining by mother correct the situation? Has she, after being upset, taught her child to respect her parental authority? No. Will she ever get the respect she deserves by complaining? Probably not. This mother is a problem sufferer.

Parental Authority

Understanding Fooling Around

One of the interpersonal relationships that can seriously impair personal authority as well as parental authority is fooling around. Everyone has done it; many children continue it until late in life.

There is the fooling around and play acting that children enjoy engaging in when relating to other children, parents or other adults. No one at this stage is using either personal, parental, or delegated authority. There is just playful human interactions.

With children, sometimes fooling around gets out of control. When this happens, one of the children, for whatever reason, uses his personal authority and says, "Stop it!" At this point his personal authority should be respected, but frequently it is not. The child then turns for protection to a parent to stop the fooling around.

Parents must teach the difference between personal authority and parental authority. If this difference is not thoroughly understood by a child, who continues uncontrollable fooling around, then he probably will not know when to stop. The situation then gets out of control. This ends the playfulness.

When personal authority is not effective, then the parent must resort to parental authority. If this is not effective, then physical strength must be used to control the situation.

If the parent fails to identify, to enforce or to explain the seriousness of disobeying parental or personal authority relationships, the parent will unwittingly help the child continue uncontrollable fooling around. The child will then have difficulty controlling other situations in the future. He must understand the need to obey authority relationships. All adults who fool around with their children should teach them the limitations of fooling around. If they don't, it will be difficult to control the child later on.

A mother frequently, when playing with her child, will not use parental authority, but will use just personal authority. This can be confusing to a child as he tries to figure out how to act and to obey. Sometimes the child gets quite bossy with mother, and she tolerates this. At other times mother will use her parental authority when this happens. Sometimes the child will lose control and mother will use parental authority. Mother usually decides for the child by the tone of her voice or by her use of words. Mother knows most of the time when to use parental, personal, or no authority at all.

Children can be taught how to make these distinctions instead of relying on mother's judgment. When relating to others outside the home, if the child knows how to evaluate authority relationships, he will make fewer mistakes in relating to others.

Teaching Essential Habits

The mother or father use parental authority, not personal authority, when teaching essential habits of self-management. These habits must be acquired. A few of these many habits are listed to show that a parent has no choice but to get a child to accept these habits. A child will not be permitted to urinate on the rug at home or in public. A child will not be permitted to use another person's property without permission. A child is not permitted to drink alcohol or to smoke. The parent has no choice but to enforce these and other essential habits upon the child.

Parental Authority

Examining Extremes

The successful mother depends upon her parental authority in teaching the essential habits of self-management to her child. How mothers enforce their parental authority ranges in varying degrees or categories between two extremes. At one extreme, the parent fails to enforce parental authority being very kind and lenient and at the other extreme, the parent is too authoritarian and harsh. Both of these extremes are damaging to a child.

Let's examine three, of many, categories to evaluate the effectiveness of parental authority in terms of learning the essential habits for acts of self-management.

1. No Enforcement of Authority: The mother who is very kind and just talks about her parental authority, but fails to enforce it, probably has a child that fails to acquire essential habits or certainly is not consistent in practicing habits. This child can be misled by mother's failure to enforce her parental authority, and he may think every person with delegated authority is weak and kind. One could expect with this misunderstanding of parental authority that there might be conflicts between teacher and child. This will be true if the teacher is not a lenient authority person. Certainly this child will not respect the personal authority of another person.

2. Enforces Authority too Strongly: The mother who is unaffectionate and enforces her parental authority strongly is strict and harsh. This mother may have a child who develops the essential habits for acts of self-management superficially. She many have a child that is rebellious and openly hates the mother, or a child who may be submissive and resentful. This child is probably counting the days until he is of age to leave home. The rebellious one in his teens may run away temporarily, but the submissive child will wish that he could. The rebellious child will have authority conflicts with teachers. Either type of child may, as an adult, reject many of the habits or acts of self-management imposed on him.

3. Moderately & Consistently Enforces Authority: The mother who affectionately enforces her parental authority moderately and consistently should have a child who easily acquires habits of self-management. Her child should have little authority difficulty with teachers and other students.

The Working Mother

Many mothers work in our society today. In "four out of ten U. S. households mothers earn the key income for their families," according to the Pew Research Center. Many mothers are also single, and are the sole breadwinners.

This does not change the role of a mother who works, but creates an additional responsibility for her. She must make time for work, time with her child, time with her husband (if married), and time for family affairs to take place. She needs to hire child care or put her child in pre-school. The age span of the child must be seriously considered. The health condition of the child is also an important factor whether mother works or not. Through all this, mothers' job has not changed in raising her child. She still needs to be a habit trainer, she still needs to teach her child the difference between personal and parental authority. She still needs to teach her child systems of self-management. She still needs to teach the five authority relationships. She still is a habit trainer. She also must bond and keep communications open with family members. Does she have time for herself? Probably not. She is a supermom and a hero in teaching self-management skills to her family. And of course, many mothers have been taught self-management skills by their parents and they have very successful households.

There are some mothers though that are so ineffective in using parental and personal authority skills that they are better off working and enrolling their child in preschool full days. The child will, at least, have a better chance to develop good habits and acts of self-management. In some limited cases it is unfortunate that the child has to go home at night to parents who undo the good that an excellent or superior teacher has done during the day. If the teacher is poor, however, the child doesn't have much of a chance to develop good self-management skills.

There are those who speak of quality time vs. full time. This can be a glib answer in some instances.

Most mothers should not work full time when they have children between the ages of three to six years of age. These are the critical years for training a child in systems of habits and acts of self-management.

Fathers Too Teach Systems Of Habits

Fathers, too, teach systems of habits and acts of self-management to children. How well they do this depends partly upon their relationships with their wives. Some wives insist that father "butt out."

Some fathers never use either their personal or parental authority. All they do is get angry or hit the child, hoping this will correct the situation. This action by father generally does not solve the problem.

Some fathers just turn the problem over to the mother.

Some fathers rely solely on their personal authority. These fathers usually do not have warm, affectionate relationships with their child and the child naturally feels insecure around father. The child obeys, but out of fear, not for reasons of understanding authority relationships and affection.

Mothers in this situation may overcompensate with affection. They may also tell the child that daddy really loves him, but this reassurance does little good for the child.

How effective mother is in exercising her parental authority depends upon her husband's authority. Some wives want to be totally dependent upon their husband's authority. Other wives are dependent upon their husband's authority because their husbands insist on it. There are wives who fret and resist their husbands' authority.

If a mother's personal and parental authority is constantly challenged by her husband, she will not be too effective in using her authority or as a habit trainer. Obviously the answer is to educate parents to use parental and personal authority so that they are both excellent habit trainers.

Husband & Wife Relationships

How well a husband and wife relate affectionately and recreationally determines how well the child will manage his life.

If they have fun with each other, their child will obviously enjoy family living.

If the parents are very serious and have little recreational time together, the child may grow up serious-minded and obviously will not have many memories of fun time spent as a family.

Parental Authority

The heavily drinking parents will obviously spoil family living for their child.

Then there is the husband and wife who just tolerate each other. When their child gets old enough, the child will stay away from home as much as possible.

How well a mother and father use parental authority, individually and in cooperation with each other, determines how well the child can shift from fooling around to managing himself and to following rules and routines.

Fathers, like mothers, can be too lenient, too harsh, and too impatient. Many fathers, however, are excellent habit trainers. Some mothers definitely will turn to fathers for their parental authority.

If mother is on the phone calling her husband whenever there is a serious authority crisis, father, after a few of these incidents, has to ignore her phone calls. This type of mother is then left helpless, as she cannot handle the situation.

By not exercising her authority, mother will certainly not help the child acquire the essential habits of self-management even if father is an excellent habit trainer. Mother is usually a full-time parent whereas father is a part-time parent. There are too many systems of habits and acts of self-management for a father to attempt to teach these in a couple of hours between seven and nine in the evening, a time of day when he and the child are tired.

Systems of habits are learned during the daytime when the child practices these habits. By encouragement, persistence, and firmness, the mother establishes the many systems of habits. She cannot depend upon father's authority at these times. Mother is the habit trainer of her child.

Quarreling

Quarreling between parents for whatever reason will not help the child acquire excellent habits of self-management. The child very likely will pick up the habits of quarreling too. It will lessen the effectiveness of parental authority and affect the emotional development of the child.

They may be loving and supportive of each other. They may both be soft spoken and very quiet. They may both be quarrelsome with rage being expressed at times.

There are so many combinations that can occur that it is difficult to predict what kind of habit trainer the couple will be. A person must know the couple and their child to determine what kind of parents they are.

Regardless of all these factors and combinations, if a mother is home all day, she is the chief habit trainer and authority trainer of the child. A husband is usually a part-time parent. If he is a traveling salesman, a busy M.D., an attorney, a businessman, or involved in any activity that requires more than forty hours per week, he may have little time for his child. Mother is then even more important as a habit trainer and an authority person.

The biggest challenge to mother's effective use of personal and parental authority is her child's personal authority and not her husband's, with some exceptions.

The time for mother to use her authority effectively is between the years of four to six. This is the time when the child acquires a lot of the essential habits.

If mother fails during this time span, her parental authority may never be as effective.

Chapter 16

Self-Management
Part I

Elements

The Framework of Self-Management that children need to learn is composed of hundreds and thousands of elements all human beings learn throughout their lifetime. The following is a list of some important elements:

> Rules
> Routines
> Decision Making
> The Five Authority Relationships
> The Four Systems of Actions and Patterns
> Time Schedules
> Completion of tasks

Elements are the building blocks that strengthen self-management, and help parents train the child to become self-managed. Gradually the child masters many of the elements over a long period of time. These elements are all around us. Parents need to be aware of them so that they can help their child use them to become self-managed.

Importance Of Rules

Why is the element of rules so important?

Rules give the child a frame of reference to follow. They prevent confusion when playing a game. There is the rule for taking turns. The rule to prevent a player from taking unfair advantage of other players. There are rules to preserve the peace of the players, etc. A parent points out to the child, over age four, while playing a game, the need for rules. This must be explained to the child. In time, the child comes to understand the necessity for rules, which is one element of the Framework of Self-Management.

Rules For Bossing Oneself

A parent again asks the child over four years of age, "Why do adults make rules?" (This is a teaching question, as the answer in the subconscious mind has not yet been recorded.)

The parent answers by saying, "So that the authority person does not have to boss you. So that a person can boss himself."

Bossing oneself, of course, is a partial answer. There are excellent reasons other than this for making rules, but basically this is the main reason for creating a rule.

Children are great enforcers of rules because they are, at times, selfish, egotistical and demanding. Any time another child tries to take an extra turn, one or more children quickly use their personal authority to force the offender to correct himself. When children are playing a game, an offender of a rule can get a lot of scolding from other children. But if there is no immediate offense to the other children, or threat or demand made on them (all selfish motives), they could care less about enforcing a rule. There are children, however, who can see that rules must be enforced whether or not they immediately impinge on them.

Rules Apply To Everyone

The highway and the family car provide an excellent example of how the adult uses the Framework of Self-Management to teach the child that rules apply to everyone. In this way, the child discovers that getting older does not let him escape from bossing himself, an important element in self-management. Rules apply to everyone.

When riding in the car, the parent tells the child to watch the signs for speed limits and to check the speedometer. This teaches the child that the parent is bossing himself on the basis of rules for highway safety which the state legislature has created.

In addition, the child is taught the value of numbers and how they are used. It is important for a child to know that a parent uses the same Framework of Self-Management that he does.

It is also important for him to know that being an adult is not a way to escape self-control.

A parent asks the child, "If the policeman catches me going too fast, what happens to me?"

The answer may be, "He will give you a ticket."

The parent asks again, "Why?"

The five-year-old will answer, "I don't know."

The parent answers, "To teach me to boss myself so that I will not hurt myself or another person. Adults get punished, too, when they do not boss themselves."

Again, the parent is getting the truth implanted in the child's subconscious mind that regardless of age, all people use a Framework of Self-Management daily.

A parent must face the reality that no one can escape punishment and should explain this to the child if a bond of trust is to be established between parent and child. A parent must explain the exceptions to the rule or else the child may not believe the rule when he sees or experiences the exception.

There are many situations in which an adult will illegally disregard a rule and not get hurt or caught. This can confuse the child unless the situation is explained.

Suppose a parent and child sees a driver running a red light. If the police are not there to catch him, he gets away with it at the time.

A parent then asks the child, "Why doesn't a driver drive through a red light at the intersection when it is safe?" (Do not expect an answer as this is a teaching question.)

The parent answers by telling the child, "If the driver did this regularly, one day he might get careless and not look both ways. Then what do you think would happen?"

The child may answer, "A car might be coming and cause an accident."

That's right. It is important to develop the habit of obeying regulations even though occasionally one could disobey without getting hurt or caught, as the incidence of getting hurt or caught are low. One may get hurt or caught one time out of twenty violations. It is that one time out of twenty when a person can get hurt or caught that causes a child or an adult to obey the regulation designed for a person's protection and the protection of others.

Children should know about these exceptions that adults make, so if you make exceptions to the rule, be sure to let the child know the odds of getting hurt or caught.

Children also know from experience that they have disobeyed a rule and have not gotten hurt or caught.

This is one of the reasons children think they do not have to obey the rule every time.

A parent must explain these exceptions so that the child will obey the rules all the time.

Immediate, Delayed, Or No Consequence

After acknowledging the situations in which the risks of getting hurt are low, the parent explains to the child that there are situations of **immediate consequences** in which one gets hurt as in touching a hot stove, drinking poison, etc.

178

Self-Management (Part I)

There are situations of **delayed consequences** that the child must also understand. It may take twenty years of excessive smoking before a person gets emphysema. However, the smoker's cough happens rather soon. Eating too much may take years before self-damage is evident. Eating too much candy every day will take time to create cavities.

Violating a rule with immediate consequence, delayed consequence, or no consequence needs to be brought to the attention of the child, as these are the three types of consequences one can experience.

Handling Defeat

Knowing that four- and five-year-olds are not able to make many decisions, parents usually buy games using dice, puzzles, or construction kits that have few pieces so that the child only has to make a few decisions.

Children, especially pre-schoolers, like to win and must be taught how to handle defeat. They eventually learn that when two play a competitive game, one of them must lose. These games are simple as there are few decisions to make and few rules to obey. If winning depends upon the roll of the dice, there is no great victory, just luck.

How Games Teach Self-Management

A parent explains to the child that he is learning to manage himself by taking turns, rolling the dice, moving the marker, and so forth.

A child needs to be told, "See, you are managing yourself. Do you understand how you are managing yourself?" This is how he learns what the word "managing" means and that he is learning self-management. The child does not know logically how he is managing himself, even though he is doing it.

The child, seven to eight, or older, wants to play games that are more complicated. He doesn't know that this means there are more complicated actions and patterns. Therefore, more decisions must be made. Accordingly, there are more rules to be learned. This is what makes these games complicated. This needs to be explained to him so that he will know why he is having difficulties. Otherwise, he will draw the false conclusion that he is inferior and may want to give up playing more complicated games.

Rule Managed vs. Mother Managed

As the garbage truck comes up the street, mother calls to her fourteen-year-old son to remind him, "Did you put out the garbage cans?"

"Oh, is it garbage day?" yells the son.

You can be sure that this mother did not train her son to boss himself on the basis of rules or routines. Otherwise, she would not need to remind him to take out the garbage. He is still "mother" managed and not "rule" managed.

"Did you do your homework?"asks father at ten p.m.

"Not yet, Dad," replies daughter.

Father then, not too gently, reminds her that on her last report card there were low grades. She too, is "parent" manged, not "rule" managed. Obviously, daughter has not established regular study times.

As mother stumbles over her five-year-old son's toys, she asks, "Dickie, how many times have I asked you to pick up your toys when you are through playing?"

Self-Management (Part I)

Dickie is not "rule" managed, but "mother" managed.

"Oh, Donna, you didn't spend that dollar on candy again. We're spending hundreds of dollars on your braces."

Another "mother" managed child. Fortunately, none of us can hear the lamenting of millions of parents over the hundreds of thousands of shirked responsibilities by sons and daughters. The litany of despair is heard in every home where there is a child who is "mother" managed.

Mother, who bears the brunt of reminding her child, would like to find some way after age four to diminish her child's dependency on her. She would like her child not to be "mother" managed, but "self" managed.

Everything in the environment — human beings, animals, plants, etc. — is governed by rules. Every day the flowers face the sun and follow it from east to west. Every launch from Cape Canaveral establishes the thousands of physical laws in the universe.

Rules and routines are the best way for any parent, officer, or group of persons to shift responsibility for control from the authority group or authority person to the individual.

A parent cannot just say to a seven-year-old, "Here is a rule or a routine. Obey it or you will be grounded for the next four weekends." If the child does not learn from the parent to be "rule" and "routine" managed, either by accident or on purpose, the child will not know how to manage himself. **It is the parent who must teach the child this process.**

Rules are one way of being self-managed and not "mother" managed.

Decision Making

A parent teaches a child that every activity has its own Framework of Self Management; such as, a baseball game, checkers, chess, tennis, cooking, traveling on freeways and surface streets, attending church or school, etc. A general framework is used in every specialized activity.

An important **element** to the Framework of Self-Management is making decisions. Decisions involve making mistakes, experiencing failure and success, defeat and victory. These emotional feelings, when making decisions, make a game exciting and yet present the greatest difficulty of self-management.

Games provide an excellent way for teaching a child that he has choices when making a decision. A child can apply this knowledge to his daily activities and other specialized activities.

Making the decision and accepting the consequences, however, are the most difficult of all the elements to teach a child. If there are many decisions to be made in a game, each decision can cost emotionally. In learning how to handle each mistake or defeat is when parental encouragement and understanding are needed. Then there is the final big emotional price to pay, defeat or victory.

System of Actions and Patterns

When a child sees a flower, a swimmer in a pool, or a goldfish in a bowl, the parent needs to point out to the child the following: In order for the flower to live and bloom, it follows a certain system of actions and patterns. In order to learn to swim, the swimmer must practice and follow a system of actions and patterns, and the same with the gold fish.

When there is a system of actions and patterns, there are rules being applied automatically.

Self-Management (Part I)

This is what a scientist knows. He watches for a consistent system of actions and patterns. If he sees this, he then discovers the rules inherent in the system of actions and patterns.

Since a child does not know that every game has a system of actions and patterns, rules, authority relationships, and decisions to be made, he must be taught to gradually name, recognize, and use these elements in the framework in order to play the game or manage any activity. The easy part is teaching a child to recognize the elements in the framework of a game.

While teaching the child to play checkers, the parent explains the **system of actions and patterns**. There are two sides: the red checkers play against the black checkers on a checkered red and black board.

The **rules** are that each player line his checkers up on the black squares only. The red squares are not used. He then explains the moves which are the **system of actions**.

It is difficult for the child, at first, to make a **decision** about which checker to move first, how to jump, and so on. He is also afraid he will make a wrong move and lose a checker. His insecurities are removed by repeating the right move many times.

The child, in the beginning, obviously has not memorized enough patterns of checker movements and has not had enough experience playing checkers to have **foresight** for a plan of attack or defense. But with enough encouragement and planned right moves by the parent, the child eventually learns how to capture checkers effectively and begins to make his own plan of attack. All of this takes time to teach the child the framework of actions when playing checkers or any game, as well as gaining the experience in playing.

183

The parent points out to the child, "See, John, in this game of checkers there is a **system of actions and patterns**. The **actions are moves** each player makes. When you move your black checkers across the board to the other side, this is an action. There are patterns for capturing a checker or checkers. You must **remember the rules** in which direction each player can move. Now you must **make a decision** which checker to move first and whether to go to the left square or to the right square. Which checker do you want to move first?"

At first the child will move his checkers in the right direction, but from lack of experience he will forget the rules and the patterns which the checkers follow. The parent then must remind the child, "What's the rule for moving checkers?" The parent then tells the child at first, "John, you can only move forward if the checker is not a king." Eventually the child will know the answer when he makes enough mistakes and is asked enough times for the right answer.

There are just countless decisions to be made when playing checkers. "Win or lose, John, one must make decisions," the parent tells him. The parent then encourages John with perhaps some planned successful moves so that he gets the idea of how to make decisions.

As a parent plays several different games, he explains the rules and other terms of the Framework of Self-Management to the child. Eventually the child will draw the conclusion that all games have a Framework of Self-Management, systems of actions, patterns, rules, decisions, and routines.

The child will also realize in time that one cannot escape the Framework of Self-Management when playing a game or doing any activity.

Chapter 17

Self-Management
Part II

The Elements Of Time

Time is another important element in the framework of self-management. The clock is an excellent impersonal boss. The child sets the alarm of the clock to boss himself. A clock can ensure regularity of action.

A week before attending first grade, a parent can buy an alarm clock so that the child can get himself up in the morning without parental help. At first, the first-grader is excited to own an alarm clock and will get up eagerly for the first few mornings to its ring.

The biggest enemy in developing the alarm clock habit for the child is the parent. The first mistake the parent makes is wanting to set the alarm clock for the child. The second mistake is letting the child stay up too late, so that the child sleeps through the ringing. The third mistake the parent makes is not putting the alarm clock far enough away from the bed so that the child must get out of bed to shut it off. The fourth mistake is not letting a child suffer real consequences for failing to get up. It seems easier for the parent to substitute nagging for real consequences.

The clock can be used in other ways to teach self-control. If a child becomes too noisy and excitable, the parent asks the child to sit still for ten minutes as a way of teaching him self-control. The parent sets a timer or an alarm clock for ten minutes. The child waits until he hears the ten minute ring before leaving the chair. This prevents the child from asking the parent several times, "Is the time up, yet?" Parents do get busy and forget. By doing this, the child knows that there will be fairness. The parent also avoids nagging.

Many years ago a mother who had four small children came to my office to solve the confusion and difficulties of the morning hours at her home.

One of the difficulties is that she did not get much work done in the morning as her children were asking for drinks, going to the bathroom, seeking her attention in many different ways, etc. She wanted to know how to solve this difficulty.

I asked her, "Do you have a fenced-in backyard?"

She answered, "Yes."

"Put all the children in the backyard for thirty minutes. Place a pitcher of water with glasses outside on the table, wall, or chair. Set the timer or alarm clock for thirty minutes so that the children will know they can come into the house for ten minutes. Then, reset the timer for ten minutes inside the house. When the timer rings, they are to go out into the yard to play for another thirty or forty minutes (If the children are responding well to this idea).

This worked for her as well as the children. The clock let the mother know how much time she had to work. It gave her time to enjoy the children during break time. The quarreling and attention-getting activities subsided. All were peaceful and happy, thanks to the clock, an important element of the framework of self-management.

When I am working at home, my five-year-old will want my attention, but there are times when I can't give him attention. Rather than put him off with excuses or to keep him from asking me periodically if I will play with him, I set the timer for ten minutes or thirty minutes. When it rings I stop and play with him. This has created an excellent relationship between both of us. He knows that I will play with him when the bell rings. He finds something to amuse himself for that short period of time.

In the evening, the child can be taught to depend on the alarm clock to notify him or her that it is time to go to bed.

There is no quarreling, no bribery or bargaining with the parent. The child just relies on the clock to boss him. Parental control is eliminated. Impersonal control is substituted. The nice part about the clock of today is that one can set it according to a.m. or p.m. Once set, it rings at the right time every evening without having to reset it. The clock has done much to improve living.

We take this mechanical device for granted. Yet, it is one of the most important mechanical devices we have. It frees us from depending upon the sun and the hour glass. It has permitted automatic control of heating, lights, water, etc. **Relating time to activities is something that a child must be taught.**

The child achieves independence by using the clock. He can become self-regulated when he creates a time schedule for himself. The child can begin to understand efficiency. He can evaluate, once he measures what he is doing, by the clock. He can decide whether time has been well spent or not.

Measuring With A Sun Dial

Although a six-year-old can read a digital clock, he should also have the experience of measuring time with a sun dial. This is the day of solar energy. Watching a sun dial, judging time by the length of a shadow in a circle is excellent training. There are so many human and plant relationships that are connected with the sun's rays. Growing plants helps the child understand time and the relationship

187

of time to the sun. An important element of every person's framework of self-management is the sun.

Understanding time and regulating oneself on the basis of time helps the child to grow out of baby misconceptions and expectations.

The Calendar (Measurement Of Time)

The calendar, a slower way of measuring time, is an important element in the framework of self-management. The clock seems more important as it is immediate. The calendar is for everyone an equally important means of independence. Every child should have not only an alarm clock in his room, but a calendar as well.

The child can begin at age five to relate activities of the day to the week and to the month. Mother puts important dates on his calendar to help him learn to measure time. In this way he can control his activities on the basis of a calendar month.

He is learning to schedule himself without knowing it. He is learning to relate his activities according to the earths rotation around the sun as well as to its daily spin of 360 degrees.

If one has a globe of the earth, a parent can show the child in relation to the sun where the globe is for December or July. A parent can also show where the globe is for morning, noon, or night. The parent can show the child how the earth moves around the sun and the moon around the earth.

Baby's Misconception Of Freedom

During the first four years baby is unaware that he controls his activities on the basis of time. What he does not know is that mother is watching not only the clock but the

188

Self-Management (Part II)

calendar too. Mother watches for the maturational development of her child by using the calendar. She uses the clock to keep him on a feeding schedule. Baby, too, is very much controlled by time. He has his own internal biological clock that regulates him, but he isn't aware of any of this.

Baby thinks that he is free to do as he pleases. He engages in aimless activity because he is too helpless to do anything else. He fusses at controlled activity. He does not like to be restrained and yet he is. Within the barriers of his environment he has limited freedom to do as he pleases. He is a victim of controlled activity, but he doesn't know it. It is his misconception of freedom that makes him fight controlled activity.

The Child's Misconception Of Freedom

Why is controlled activity not enjoyable to a child? Like the baby, a child cannot control his body for too long a span of time. His attention span is also short.

The child doesn't like the uncomfortable body movements that he must at first accept like holding a bat, catching ball in a mitt or putting the right fingers on the right keys on a piano or musical instrument. He doesn't like the pressure of an adult forcing him to keep learning an activity until he can do it. He doesn't like the repeated experience of failures before he can succeed. He feels inferior. He is not sure what he should do. He prefers his accidental ways of learning. This preserves his feelings of omnipotence.

At six years, a child prefers random activities to taught and supervised activities; although the five-year-old occasionally enjoys supervised activities. The antagonism of controlled activity can increase or decrease, depending upon the skills of the parent or the teacher.

189

If the parent, however, resents controlled activity, he will be against teaching his child controlled activity. Some parents have not given up the idea that random activity is better than controlled activity.

A favorite way of getting out of controlled activity with all its natural frustration is to not do it. The child knows that this is a sure way of solving a frustration. Don't do it. So the older child says as an excuse to avoid frustration, "I don't have time to do it." He thus procrastinates.

Time (An Element of Self-Management)

All activities will, in time, cause the child to think in a time frame. Time is an element of self-management. It is a part of the Framework of Self-Management. Self-regulation on the basis of a time schedule will take years to master.

By ten and eleven years of age, a child can do simple time and motion studies which help him better accept controlled living when he sees how much more he can get done.

The child becomes easier to live with as he understands how to get more free time by doing an activity faster. If he wastes emotional energy complaining, hopefully he eventually learns a job will get done faster without complaining.

A child should, in time, come to understand that adult living means living by a schedule in an orderly manner.

Seventy-Two Hours Of Leisure Time

At about ten, a parent should train a child to know how many hours there are in a week. An adult may not know this and accordingly does not plan his time as to how many hours there are in a week. Some adults may resent scheduling themselves this way.

When one has listened to as many children and teenagers as I have complaining about their school work and

Self-Management (Part II)

chores, you know that mother or father has not taught these children about the use of time. So I patiently, time after time, solve all this complaining by teaching the child that he has forty hours of free time after school hours, Monday through Friday.

By asking children or teenagers for an hourly account of their time after school, I found that not any of them could give me an accurate idea of what they did. They complained when asked to do something because they didn't have time.

When it is pointed out to them that they have seventy-two unscheduled hours a week, they then begin to see how little enjoyment they receive from their free hours and how little they have accomplished. They also begin to realize that no one is going to feel sorry for them when they complain or waste their own precious time.

In addition to the forty hours of unscheduled activities. Monday through Friday, a child has thirty-two hours of free time on the weekends.

It is well for parents to think of these seventy-two unscheduled hours so that one doesn't get to feeling sorry for their child.

It is necessary for a child to learn to be happily busy, rather than to be pressured into doing an activity. To keep busy happily is the goal for every human being. The time to learn to do this is during the childhood years.

A parent can frequently quote to a child that he has seventy-two hours of free time when not attending classes. It forces both of them to evaluate what the child is doing with his free time, or what I prefer to call leisure time.

Setting Priorities By Time
Time also involves another element of self-manage-

Chapter 17

ment; that is, priority scheduling. Setting priorities by time is absolutely necessary for adult living.

This is a way of organizing oneself according to priorities or sequences of activities. First, one wakes up, showers, dresses, eats breakfast, makes the bed and goes to school. This is another way of not being "mother" managed. Seniority is a part of priority. Older children have privileges that younger children do not have. This creates for the younger child an incentive to look forward to his older brother's priority rights when he is older.

Generalizations

Generalizations are an important element of the framework of self-management.

There is a **management vocabulary** that a child must know in order to be able to organize himself. It is important to teach these management words and to be sure that the child understands them. These words are **theories of self-management** and parents teach these theories, too. Words and theories are part of the framework of self-management.

Every person, whether baby or senior, manages themselves on the basis of **concepts** and **generalizations.** This is so taken for granted that many adults are not aware of generalizations. This may be the most important element of the framework of self-management. It is also an extremely important part of self-organization.

As soon as baby starts to use words, he begins to organize himself on the basis of generalizations. He was doing this before he spoke words, but it is far easier to adjust to the environment with words.

The child is constantly creating statements or generalizations. He tests his statements immediately in order to know

Self-Management (Part II)

how to adjust to many situations and other people. This is a part of self-management. Since he has had little training so far in self-management, he may come up with wrong or comic statements which need to be corrected by an adult.

Sometimes a parent corrects these generalizations of the child without the child ever knowing that he is being corrected for his generalization. The adult must let the child know that this is what he is being corrected for.

A two-year-old calls a banana an orange. Mother says, "No. It is yellow and we call it a banana, not an orange. You made a wrong generalization." Mother lets the child know that it was the generalization that she was correcting.

The three-year-old says the "balloon falls down," meaning the air has escaped and the balloon has fallen to the ground. The parent corrects the generalization.

Parents are not always thinking carefully through the generalizations that they are teaching their child. Mother, when exasperated, will say, "Oh, you will never learn it. Forget it."

Words of permanency (such as, always, never, everytime, all, none, and everyone) are words that a child should be taught to use with care. These words usually cause false generalizations to be drawn.

Mothers many times use **words of degree** (such as frequently, often, seldom, few, or almost). Children should be taught to use these **words of degree** as they more accurately describe a situation. Generalizations that contain these words are more apt to be true.

Parents also correct the child from using **inappropriate statements.**

A child will say, "I hate peas."

The parent corrects the child and says, "You made a generalization about peas. Why is this not a correct generalization?"

This is a learning situation so the child will not know the answer the first time you ask this type of question so you tell him. "A person cannot hate peas, but he can dislike them."

Children control themselves on the basis of generalizations. A few examples are:

"Don't walk across a busy intersection unless the light is green."

"Don't stare at the sun, you will hurt your eyes."

There are hundreds of such statements that a child learns for self-protection or self-management. How well a child controls himself on the basis of generalizations depend upon how well he understands the three consequences:

> immediate consequence
> delayed consequence
> no consequence

These consequences usually accompany a generalization.

There are all kinds of special frameworks (such as art, math, gardening, reading, games, etc.) that require human beings to adjust to each special framework. How many special frameworks are there? There may be thousands.

The one general framework of self-management that every child must learn is to survive happily. No parent can do less than teach this general framework to a child. If the child masters the elements of that framework, he can adjust very well to other frameworks.

This Is A Mature Adult

FRANCIS H. WISE, PH.D. 1973

A Person:

who can organize time
>Is an efficient adult;

who protects animals, human beings, plants, and
property
>Is a humane and loving adult;

who can disagree pleasantly and effectively
>Is a peaceful adult;

who can give attention and who can listen
>Is a wise adult and a good conversationalist;

who can be considerate of another person
>Is a thoughtful and appreciative adult;

who knows how to achieve goals
>Is a successful adult;

who knows how to control his body
>Is a healthy adult;

who knows how to be self-entertaining
>Is never a lonely adult;

who knows and can live within his limitations
>Is not a frustrated adult;

who knows how to forgive
>Is a loved and loving individual;

who is not afraid to defend himself
>Will not be a humiliated adult;

who is not afraid to be hurt
>Will not be a fearful adult;

who is not afraid to die
>Is a serene adult;

who can worship
>Is an orderly adult;

A Person:

who can sacrifice
> Will be a leader of adults;

who can save
> Need not fear old age

who pays his bills on time;
> Is not a harassed adult;

who truly knows how to learn from his mistakes
> Is not an opinionated adult, but a child of God;

who understands the purpose of authority
> Is a cooperative adult;

who accepts routines, rules, and laws of a group —
> be it family, club, school, church, or state
> Is a harmonious adult;

who can control himself through routines, rules, and laws
> Is an independent adult;

who can accept standardized patterns of living
> Is a respected adult;

who can accept changes and difficulties in daily living
> Is a stable adult;

who can control his behavior upon the basis of generalizations
> Is an intelligent adult;

who can control his feelings
> Is a happy adult;

who can enjoy living
> Has mastered these skills and is

A Mature Adult

The Ten Commandments

1. Do not have any other gods before Me.

2. You shall not make any graven image, or any likeness of anything that is in heaven above or that is in the earth beneath or that is in the water under the earth.

3. You shall not take the Name of the Lord our God in vain.

4. Remember the sabbath day, to keep it holy.

5. Honor your father and your mother.

6. You shall not kill.

7. You shall not commit adultery.

8. You shall not steal.

9. You shall not bear false witness against your neighbor.

10. You shalt not covet your neighbor's house, wife, nor anything that is your neighbor's.

INDEX

INDEX

INDEX

INDEX

INDEX

INDEX

Become Involved to be successful!

Memorization

Teachers explain the multiplication tables to children. They also show them how to solve problems. Many children practice solving lots of problems in a workbook by the hundreds of combinations. Yet, so many children do not make the answers and the combinations automatic as the child does not know how to teach himself. He is doing what he is asked to do without involving himself beyond writing down the answers and getting the work done. Eventually a parent will have to force the child to become involved enough to give the answers to the combinations automatically. This is called memorization. In order to memorize anything, the child must become involved in what he is doing.

www.ingramcontent.com/pod-product-compliance
Lightning Source LLC
Chambersburg PA
CBHW051957090426
42741CB00008B/1432